THE
PRESIDENTIAL
CAMPAIGN

THE
PRESIDENTIAL
CAMPAIGN

☆ ☆ ☆ ☆ ☆ ☆ ☆ ☆ ☆ ☆ ☆ ☆ ☆ ☆ ☆

*The Leadership Selection Process
after Watergate*

An *essay by* STEPHEN HESS

THE BROOKINGS INSTITUTION
Washington, D.C.

Library of Congress Cataloging in Publication Data:
Hess, Stephen.
  The Presidential campaign.
  Bibliography: p.
  1. Presidents—United States—Election.   I. Title.
JK528.H45   329'.01'0973   74-1433
ISBN 0-8157-3589-8

9 8 7 6 5 4 3 2 1

Foreword

THE STYLE AND FORM of political campaigns have changed remarkably little since the end of the nineteenth century when William Jennings Bryan and Mark Hanna invented a "new politics" for conducting the presidential canvass. Most politicians and many journalists have taken it for granted that American presidents would continue to be chosen through the same rituals that have served in the past. Scholars, too, have tended to accept the traditional modes of campaigning and have turned their attention to other areas of inquiry. The presidential campaign as a field of study has been neglected at least partly because scholars, from the beginning of the New Deal until the escalation of the war in Vietnam, have found the process by which presidents are chosen to be generally satisfactory.

But times have changed. This essay is published during a period of growing discontent with the way presidential campaigns are conducted, with the costs of campaigns, and with the manner in which the substance of campaigns is communicated, both by the news media and the contenders. It is therefore appropriate to ask questions about the attributes Americans expect in a President and the functions a presidential campaign is expected to perform.

This is the starting-point of Stephen Hess's investigation. He goes on to assess how effectively the presidential selection process chooses acceptable candidates, develops issues, and gives the voters information upon which rational decisions can be based. The essay concludes with his proposals for corrective action.

Stephen Hess is a Brookings senior fellow. He views his subject not only as a student of American presidential politics but as a participant in a number of recent presidential campaigns during which he worked on party platforms and traveled with candidates for the presidency.

The author expresses his appreciation to the following persons for commenting on drafts of this manuscript: David S. Broder, Thomas E. Cronin, Max Frankel, Erwin Hargrove, John H. Kessel, Richard P. Nathan, Judith H. Parris, Gilbert Y. Steiner, and James L. Sundquist. He also appreciates the services at Brookings of Robert Erwin, editorial associate, and Rosa Cook, secretary.

The opinions expressed in this essay are those of the author and should not be ascribed to the trustees, officers, or other staff members of the Brookings Institution.

KERMIT GORDON
President

May 1974
Washington, D.C.

Contents

☆ ☆ ☆ ☆ ☆ ☆ ☆ ☆ ☆ ☆ ☆ ☆ ☆ ☆ ☆ ☆ ☆

ONE Introduction

☆ ☆ ☆ ☆ ☆ ☆ ☆ ☆ ☆ ☆ ☆ ☆ ☆ ☆ ☆ ☆ ☆

SOMEWHERE in this land of 211 million cit-
izens we must assume there are persons capable of providing
presidential leadership within a democratic context, sensitive
to the restraints of power, ambitious to promote the public
good, skillful in the exercise of constitutionally given responsibilities, experienced in the management of large undertakings,
calm and reassuring in character and style, with a measured
view of national needs and world realities.

If so, the way we go about finding them becomes of crucial
importance. A restatement of presidential *qualities* is one way
of holding a mirror to the selection process. For the method
by which Presidents are picked is a testing; it serves the same
purpose as any technique designed to screen and select among
applicants for a job. Thus the first task of this essay is to ask
whether there are presidential qualities that are particularly
appropriate and useful in discharging the duties of office.
Chapter 2 attempts to describe the qualities that transcend
the temporal and the ideological, that can fit a conservative
President as comfortably as a liberal President, that can apply
in periods of social change and conflict as well as in periods
that demand consolidation and restoration of order. The
proper mix of talents will be different at different times, but
the ingredients will be the same. Only when we assay what is
desirable can we judge whether we are testing for the desirable
and how well designed is the test. The campaign is not an
end in itself. Voters in a democratic society are expected to
partake in this quadrennial exercise, tedious and even de-

grading as it may be, so as to gather clues about the acceptability of the contestants; if the clues are not forthcoming or
if the clues are misleading, then the system fails in its primary
obligation. If, on the other hand, the voters are presented
with sufficient information and are able to register their decision, then the system meets one criterion of success even if
it may be esthetically unpleasing or if subsequent events prove
that the electorate was not attentive enough.

It is perfectly possible to have a system that works well in
probing the assets and liabilities of those who offer themselves
to the electorate, yet fails to produce a sufficient pool of talent
from which to make the selection. Chapter 3, on *availability*,
asks whether the political system produces "enough" and the
"right" sorts of candidates, this being quite distinct from the
issue of whether the system properly tests those candidates
whom it produces.

The campaign is primarily a process of personnel selection.
But it is more than the electorate operating as a gigantic
search committee. The campaign also serves as corrective, the
righting of perceived wrongs; as policy formulation, the proposal and approval of issue positions; as national self-examination; and as entertainment. The purpose of Chapter 4 is to
explore these *functions* of the campaign and to evaluate how
well they are performed in the American system.

Two other areas are of special concern when trying to
judge the continuing utility of a system that was originally
tailored to a smaller and less diversified population in a technologically simpler century:

• What are the influences and effects of television and
other changes in communications on the presidential selection process? When the electorate receives its information in
new ways and when the candidates deliver their messages in
new ways, new possibilities for distortion creep into the system. Chapter 5, on *communications*, examines the mass
media both as voter-informing and candidate-advertising
vehicles.

• Can a method of raising and regulating money in politics be devised that will encourage good people to run for office, eliminate corruption, and create a healthier political climate? The national reaction to Watergate has created a unique opportunity for enacting corrective legislation, which is discussed in Chapter 6, on money.

A functional system of leadership selection must produce an adequate supply of talented people seeking the office; test the qualities that a successful President must have; expose those qualities that a President should not have; present the electorate with issues of substance; and provide sufficient opportunity to appraise both candidates and issues. Did the system fail in 1972? In revisiting the system in light of Watergate, Chapter 7 (the concluding chapter) offers an agenda for change.

TWO Presidential Qualities

☆ ☆ ☆ ☆ ☆ ☆ ☆ ☆ ☆ ☆ ☆ ☆ ☆ ☆ ☆ ☆

*What are the qualities that transcend the
temporal and the ideological, that can fit a
conservative President as comfortably as a
liberal President, that can apply in periods of
social change and conflict as well as in periods
that demand consolidation and restoration
of order? The proper mix of talents will be
different at different times, but the ingredients
will be the same. Only when we assay what
is desirable can we judge whether we are testing
for the desirable . . .*

A PRESIDENT of the United States must be
prepared to become a *public person*. This means more than
holding public office and assuming public responsibilities.
Public, in this sense, means exposed: becoming a public property, different only in degree from the White House in which
the President sleeps and works and may have to raise children.
The people have the right of inspection, and those places that
are put off-limits are automatically suspect. The experience
may be akin to having one's life opened for a perpetual house-
and-garden tour, with a steady stream of strangers passing
through, fingering the furniture as well as the presidential ego.

The loss of privacy is near total. When a President is ill,
his bodily functions will be the subject of press briefings; his
friends become celebrities by definition; his family a monu-
ment on which the public can scrawl graffiti; even his dog is
the First Dog of the Land. This extension of the presidency

4

to include the President's private life is a twentieth-century phenomenon; there is nothing comparable in the earlier history of the country. It is a by-product of technological breakthroughs in communications.[1] As the means and capacity to distribute information increased, and as the information business became highly profitable, the President, his family, and his friends were turned into a major source of the raw material that fueled a major industry. The trend is irreversible.

Any description of the political techniques employed by a President would differ little from those of the corporation executive, union leader, or academic administrator. Each, in essentially the same manner, offers rewards or withholds rewards, with varying degrees of subtlety; each, in essentially the same manner, assesses the strengths and weaknesses of supporters and opponents; each seeks ways to build constituencies and to minimize opposition. What does differ is the public aspect of presidential politics. The politics of business, union, and university are essentially private—played out within the confines of board room, union hall, and faculty commons. The United States Senate provides a public platform for its members, but Senate politics, conducted in cloakroom and conference committee, is essentially private. Only the President must have the ability to conduct his business without a hiding place. Thus the presidential quality of being a public person, which assumes a willingness to violate one's sense of privacy, becomes essential to the operation of democratic government. No open society can afford a privatized presidency. The openness of the presidential office is the best insurance that there will be no dark corners in which Watergate-type corruption can breed and that public policy will be properly ventilated before being approved.

A President must have *high intelligence*: receptivity to new ideas, ability to absorb complex thoughts, capacity to distill

1. See Daniel J. Boorstin, "Selling the President to the People: The Direct Democracy of Public Relations," *Commentary* (November 1955), pp. 421–27.

ideas to their essence. This raises the question of what specific knowledge a President should have in order to perform his duties. Theodore Sorensen said in 1963: "To make informed decisions, the President must be at home with a staggering range of information. . . . He must know all about the ratio of cotton acreage to prices, of inventory accumulations to employment, of corporate investment to earnings, of selected steel prices to the economy, and of the biological effects of fall-out to the effects of natural radiation."[2] The intellectual superman image of the presidency is unfair to the man in the White House and to the electorate. It is unattainable and untrue that a President need know "all about" an almost infinite range of recondite matters, any more than a university chancellor need know all about macroeconomics, clinical psychology, microbiology, and linguistics in order to run his institution. What a President need know is whose advice to seek: can one person give him full and dispassionate information, or need he seek out competing experts? Which subjects are important now, and which may be important in the near future? Must he make a decision? What might be the consequences if no decision is made or if a decision is made by someone else? These, rather than "the ratio of cotton acreage to prices," are the sorts of things that a President need know.

Yet Sorensen is correct if what he means is that a President's intelligence must be broadly based. Above all, a President should be a person of *wide interests and concerns*. The problems of the country are diverse and interrelated. A President has to respond to particular crises as they arise, and often he must compartmentalize his attention to conform with certain governmental timetables—there is a time to prepare a budget, a time to deliver the Economic Report to the Congress, and so forth. Nevertheless, it is only his ability to keep many balls in the air that can harmonize national needs

2. Theodore E. Sorensen, *Decision-Making in the White House* (Columbia University Press, 1963), pp. 38–39.

and aspirations. Richard Nixon's performance provides an interesting example of misallocation of time. He is a man of high intelligence but narrow interests. During his first term he became almost totally consumed with matters of foreign policy. This was not the reason for Watergate, but it was the prime reason for the way he organized his White House, which, in turn, helped to create Watergate. In overdelegating responsibilities that were not directly related to foreign policy he abandoned the oversight of activities in which corruption then developed. Bill Moyers suggests that misallocation of time also occurred in the Johnson White House during the winter of 1965, when the crucial decisions were made to escalate the war in Vietnam: "The President was—we were all—caught up in presenting the Great Society legislation to Congress. . . . Vietnam seemed to be more of a nuisance than a menace."[3]

Depending on which problems most urgently call for attention in a given period, however, a President can benefit from the expertise he brings to the office. Eisenhower's military background was often disparaged; still, when the problem was how to make cuts in the defense budget during the post-Korean War period, a President who had been a five-star general was uniquely suited for the task.[4] Especially in the area of foreign policy—given the speed of events, the potential gravity of acting or not acting, the secrecy often required, and

3. "Bill Moyers Talks about LBJ," *Atlantic* (July 1968), p. 30. Richard Tanner Johnson suggests the same sort of misallocation of time under President Kennedy: "Kennedy, viewing Berlin as his *big* problem, perhaps did not have a great deal of residual energy to invest in staffing out Vietnam." *Managing the White House* (Harper and Row, 1974), p. 148. See also p. 147 in this same book.

4. What also may be at work here is what I have called "the bendoverbackwards factor" in politics. Not only would Eisenhower have lost a popularity contest at the Pentagon by the end of his presidential term, but John Kennedy may well have been, as Murray Kempton predicted he would become, the most anticlerical chief executive since Millard Fillmore. See Stephen Hess, "Is There a Republican Approach to Government?" *Washington Monthly* (February 1969), p. 59.

the degree to which his powers are unchallenged—a chief executive will be particularly advantaged by specialized knowledge. Lyndon Johnson had little experience with or interest in foreign affairs when he came to office. In his handling of the Vietnam War, the problem was not that the President received one type of advice exclusively. While the Defense Department pressured for increased expenditures and involvement, it is now clear from the Pentagon Papers that the CIA consistently reported that the war was not going well and was an essentially political struggle. Perhaps U.S. commitments in Vietnam might have been of a different order if Johnson had had a background more suited to weighing the competing advice he was given.

Intelligence should not be confused with intellectuality, which need not be a presidential quality. Indeed, an intellectual may be at some disadvantage in the White House. The intellectual may have difficulty translating thoughts into the common idiom; or may be removed by class and background and experience from the immediate concerns that people expect a President to handle; or may be incapable of taking prompt action because of a disinclination to base decisions on imperfect information or to reduce complexities to terms that can be dealt with in the political process.[5] Then, too, the intellectual may seek advice primarily from others who are equally quick of mind. This probability is hardly an argument that mediocrity also deserves a place at the high table, but it serves as a reminder that the kind of wisdom so valuable to Presidents often is possessed by those whose talents

5. Commenting on the historian as political activist, Keith Robbins contends that the historian's "very knowledge of the complexity of circumstances may inhibit him when he has to decide. As a historian, he knows there is so much to be said for both sides that as a politician he is paralysed." See "History and Politics: The Career of James Bryce," *Journal of Contemporary History* (July–October 1972), p. 38. Contrast this with Truman's decision to use the atomic bomb: "Let there be no mistake about it. I regarded the bomb as a military weapon and never had any doubt that it should be used." Harry S. Truman, *Year of Decisions* (Doubleday, 1955), p. 419.

are not readily apparent when they open their mouths. Sometimes dazzling brilliance more quickly gets an administration into trouble than the type of sensitivity that "Uncle Joe" Cannon felt comes from those politicians whose ears are full of grasshoppers because they are so close to the ground. The best definition of the democratic statesman remains Bagehot's "an uncommon man of common opinions."[6]

A President must have a transcending *honesty.* After a period of corruption, integrity may be sufficient reason to elect a person—and the act of being honest may become an important public service—but honesty is not greatness; it is only necessary. The same principle applies to *courage.* A President must have the courage to swim against the tide, the courage to take unpopular actions, and the courage not to act, which sometimes can be the greatest courage of all. But Presidents also can make courageously bad decisions.

A President must have a *feel of the nation*—what are the people's hopes, what are their fears—and a strong sense of the concrete. A President must understand that he presides over a large body of individuals and that his policies will affect people one by one.

Yet almost everything that happens once a new President steps inside the White House makes it difficult for him to consider individual reactions. His information will be collectivized for him. The goods that workers produce and the services they perform become the gross national product. People become the raw data for tabulations, percentages, and trends. What a President is to know of the American people he must learn before he becomes President. Once he is surrounded by the Secret Service and the Signal Corps and the reporters assigned to "cover" him, he will continue to be seen by the people, and occasionally he even can be touched by them. He still will learn about them, primarily through the media and from his advisers, both inside and outside of gov-

6. Quoted in Harold J. Laski, *The American Presidency* (Harper, 1940), p. 37.

ernment. But he will stop learning from them. For this reason it is essential that the selection process be as close to the people as possible and that it be a learning experience for future Presidents.

It is a President's *political antennae* that will tell him whether he has to inch his way toward a goal or whether he will be able to strike boldly, how flexible he will have to be and how to best deploy his powers to gain the support he needs. There is a sharp cutting edge to the political qualities that we expect in our Presidents. We expect them to maneuver, compromise, arm-twist, threaten—all in our best interests. Thus standards of presidential behavior differ markedly from those we value in our personal relations. It is a hard point for us to bring into harmony with ethical teachings. Of all twentieth-century Presidents, the two Roosevelts came closest to having the kinds of political qualities that allowed them to perform their duties most effectively.[7] Both were seekers of power with a single-minded intensity, experts at manipulation, with the ability to quickly reverse field. We might have desired them to be persons of inestimable goodness as was William Howard Taft. But it was advantageous to the nation that the Roosevelts were master politicians, whereas Taft's personal goodness proved only modestly useful in the absence of the political skills necessary to operate successfully.

The Roosevelts also were strongly exhibitionistic. All Presidents do not have to have their well-developed dramatic instincts and their appreciation of the mysteries of making news. But all Presidents must find ways to *communicate*, to persuade the people and to arouse and enlist support. The ability to use the White House to create consensus, ease fears, and restore confidence assumes a *style* that is acceptable to a majority of the people. Past presidential styles have been too wide-ranging to permit easy generalization. At different times

7. See Erwin C. Hargrove, *Presidential Leadership* (Macmillan, 1966), p. 146.

we have accepted leadership from the laconic Coolidge, the boyishly exuberant Kennedy, and the calm grandfatherly Eisenhower.

But at a minimum, presidential style assumes a background that is without serious blemishes or, since there is a sort of statute of limitations in politics, only blemishes of ancient vintage that have been expiated or excused by the electorate. Despite the Mrs. Grundy image of America as a nation of official puritans, the country has consistently shown a sophisticated view of sexual conduct as a potential disqualification for the presidency. Comments and speculation on intimate relationships have sometimes figured in presidential campaigns (Jefferson, Jackson, Cleveland, Wilson), but never has that aspect been a determining factor. Shady financial dealings have been far more decisive, as best illustrated by the Cleveland-Blaine contest of 1884 in which Cleveland was accused of fathering a bastard and Blaine was accused of receiving a veiled bribe from a railroad. The voters chose Cleveland.[8]

A President can wear loud sport shirts or lose his temper at a music critic. (Such actions might increase his popular standing if they are perceived as immaterial to doing those things which are presidential.) Decorum is not automatically equated with solemnity or middle-class behavior. While we are basically a middle-class country, we have elected and taken pride in a collection of quite patrician Presidents. A President need not be like us. Sometimes it may help him if he is not, if only because we think it less likely that a rich man will

8. The reasoning of the voters was perhaps reflected in the words of a man from Chicago at the time: "I gather that Mr. Cleveland has shown high character and great capacity in public office but that in private life his conduct has been open to question, while on the other hand, Mr. Blaine in public life has been weak and dishonest while he seems to have been an admirable husband and father. The conclusion that I draw from these facts is that we should elect Mr. Cleveland to the public office which he is so admirably qualified to fill and remand Mr. Blaine to private life which he is so eminently fitted to adorn." Quoted in Sidney Hyman, "Scandal Following Script," *Washington Post*, Oct. 18, 1964; also see D. W. Brogan, *Politics in America* (Harper, 1954), p. 250.

steal from the public till. A show of wealth does not offend most of us, perhaps because most of us would like to be wealthy or because we may think that wealth imparts special talents to those who have "made it" or good omens to those who have been born with it—especially since the rich, by the act of seeking elective office, are asking to serve us.

The electorate has a right to expect certain executive talents in every President.[9] He is the manager of a vast enterprise. The executive qualities that are presidential primarily have to do with skills at choosing personnel and methods of arriving at decisions. Some people can make up their minds about complex matters faster than others. There are instincts —and a dash of good luck—that enable some executives to pick the right people for the right jobs. They know how to find advisers who compensate for their own weaknesses. They have a genius for getting people to work together for a common cause. There is a touch of toughness that we expect in a President. How, for example, does he discipline subordinates for alleged wrongdoing?

The President as executive must choose those decisions that he wishes to make. He cannot possibly make all decisions in an undertaking that employs over five million persons. He must not be "nibbled to death by the guppies of minor or marginal issues."[10] Nor can he allow himself to be overtaken by events and swept along by the actions of subordinates. He should populate the White House with persons capable of sorting out problems for his attention; he should appoint

9. Most scholars, on the contrary, have downgraded the need for executive talents in the White House. James MacGregor Burns goes so far as to completely separate "leadership" from "management." Leaders, he thinks, should be concerned with "goals rather than methods"; executive qualities are "secondary matters." See *Presidential Government* (Houghton Mifflin, 1966), pp. 194–95. None of the seven presidential qualities singled out by Clinton Rossiter are executive. See *The American Presidency* (rev. ed., Mentor Books, 1960), pp. 172–74. The reason for this treatment may be that management is outside the competence of those of us who regularly assess the presidency.

10. Bryce N. Harlow in Emmet John Hughes, *The Living Presidency* (Coward, McCann and Geoghegan, 1973), p. 342.

department and agency heads who can manage their operations effectively and represent him faithfully to the Congress, the bureaucracy, and their constituents. He must resist the temptation of allowing the White House to become "operational," and he must resist being captured by the departments' perceptions of reality. He must arrive at decisions and make them known in ways that do not undermine those on whom he must rely to carry them out; at the same time, he must prod his appointees and the civil service to provide better information, more efficient operations, and more humane services. All of this he must do without the tools that most executives have in the private sector. For he manages an undertaking that responds more to persuasion than to hierarchal command, whose ultimate funding is not under his control, and whose employees are largely outside his power to hire and fire.

The political executive needs great *stamina*. A new school of counter-wisdom contends that "no President ever died of overwork." George Reedy graphically reminds us that the nation makes a President's days as painless as staff, technology, and creature comforts allow.[11] (Historically the point is well taken. James K. Polk came closest to working himself to death, and even he survived his presidential term.)[12] Still, we elect a President to run the executive branch of government, and we expect him to have the energy to match the task.

A more subtle presidential quality is a *sense of history*. Not a reliance on history "to make the most of precedents established by his predecessors, and to see in the problems confronting him replicas of problems confronting chief executives in the past."[13] For precedents are wondrously available

11. George F. Reedy, *The Twilight of the Presidency* (World, 1970), pp. 4, 21.
12. Thomas A. Bailey has shown that, when assassinations are factored out, our Presidents have lived beyond their actuarial life expectancy. See *Presidential Greatness* (Appleton-Century, 1966), pp. 340–43.
13. Joseph E. Kallenbach, *The American Chief Executive* (Harper and Row, 1966), pp. 265–66.

to buttress most any position, and history repeats itself only in the most general terms. Rather, a sense of history provides the understanding of what must be preserved and protected in the country, such as individual freedom, human dignity, and political democracy. It is an understanding of history that locates for a President where he fits into the constitutional scheme of things, which keeps him in phase with the other forces in government so that he operates as neither steamroller nor pushover in his relations with the Congress, courts, and states. In this sense, a President's understanding of history becomes a restraint on despotism.

This historical sense also should provide the perspective to resist fads and passions of the moment. Unfortunately, the "exalting" presidential "thought that he sits in Lincoln's seat" (Clinton Rossiter's wording) is capable of producing a touch of megalomania. American history, with its play of fortuity, should be more humbling.

The ultimate usefulness of a President's personal qualities is to *inspire public trust*. This is not the same as being loved or noncontroversial. Nor can it be defined solely by style or personality, although style and personality can help inspire trust; nor by programs or ideologies, although these too help inspire trust. It does not mean trust by everyone, an impossibility, but trust by enough to ensure that the social fabric will remain intact and that some effective actions can be taken.[14]

The elements that go into inspiring trust are a style that is not offensive to the majority, a transcending honesty, a high level of intelligence, a willingness to deal with the "real"

14. John Reed, "Pomp and Politician," New York Times, Dec. 8, 1972, equates trust with lack of pomp. One way to establish trust would be to "abolish the 21-gun salutes, the honor guards, the red carpets, the elaborate state dinners, the Presidential hideaways." Even assuming a certain literary overkill on Reed's part, there is no evidence that pomp has anything to do with trust for most Americans. The contrary may even be true: the ceremonial has a long history. Excessive pomp is not the reason that Herbert Hoover or Lyndon Johnson lost trust; disposing of presidential yachts by Kennedy and Nixon did not measurably affect the people's trust in them one way or another.

problems that immediately touch people's lives, a sense of patriotism, and a public confidence in those to whom a President lends his prestige and authority.[15] What we expect in a President we also expect in those around him, only to a lesser degree. This encompasses the First Family and his associates in descending order of importance down to members of his political party.

Finally, to aspire to more than adequacy, a President must dream grandly. He should have goals and direction and, if possible, some concrete proposals upon taking office. Yet this is not necessary for every President. There are moments that call for marking time. The consolidationist President has a necessary role to play. One problem with many theories of the presidency is the assumption that all Presidents must be "heroic" and must interpret their "powers with maximum liberality."[16] But every President should desire to leave the

15. The Kennedy campaign of 1960 was based largely on the sense of patriotism referred to here. "I don't believe that there is anything this country cannot do," John Kennedy said in the final televised debate. "I don't believe there's any burden or any responsibility that any American would not assume to protect his country."

A presidential candidate can praise the country and not be believed; or he can fault the country, though this is tricky ground and requires sure footing. Ultimately, however, the electorate must feel that a candidate deeply respects his country. Though a certain "anti-patriotism dogma" exists, its advocacy will not elect a President or aid him in performing his duties. One result of the new skepticism is that until recently a President had to prove that he was not trustworthy: the people were willing to assume the best. Now the reverse is probably true.

16. See Louis W. Koenig, *The Chief Executive* (rev. ed., Harcourt, Brace and World, 1968), pp. 11–12; Arthur M. Schlesinger, Jr., *The Crisis of Confidence* (Houghton Mifflin, 1969), p. 298; and James MacGregor Burns, *Uncommon Sense* (Harper and Row, 1972), p. 172. This view of the "strong, heroic" President largely was based on scholars' infatuation with Franklin Roosevelt and was particularly in vogue during the 1950s and early 1960s. Beginning with the steep escalation of the Vietnam War in 1965 there has been a gradual reassessment of the presidential office. See Reedy, *The Twilight of the Presidency*; Henry Fairlie, *The Kennedy Promise* (Doubleday, 1973); Eugene J. McCarthy, *The Year of the People* (Doubleday, 1969), esp. pp. 294–95; and Barbara W. Tuchman, "Should We Abolish The Presidency?" *New York Times*, Feb. 13, 1973.

nation better than he finds it; every President should be able to push to some degree against the limits of what is considered feasible; and every President should have a generosity of spirit that seeks to bring out what is best in the people.

In assessing how well these qualities are tested by our selection process it is useful to consider the presidential campaign as having three essential characteristics. It is based on the law of contradictions. It is quintessentially political. It is intensely personal.

The law of contradictions assumes that each candidate makes the arguments that he feels will place him in the best light and that he is under no obligation to state the weaknesses of his position or the strengths of his opponents. *Truth* may be on neither side of an argument, on both sides, or partly on both sides. Campaigns, from the viewpoint of the candidates, are not about truth per se but are expected to produce an approximation of truth through the clash of contending forces.

This adversary system is not well designed to inspire trust in future Presidents, create honest dialogue, or even encourage a candidate to dream grandly.[17] With each candidate

17. It might be useful to speculate why the adversary process apparently works well in jurisprudence and not well in politics. There are at least six differences between the courtroom and the campaign. In the courtroom the issues are limited and carefully prescribed; the number of players are few; the traditions of behavior and standards of admissibility are established beforehand and are enforceable; the verdict is usually negotiable; the advocates—lawyers, not defendants—are relatively disinterested parties; and the decision is based on a determination of fact or law. None of these factors exists in the adversary proceedings of politics: the issues are whatever each side and the outside players choose, and rarely are they the same for each side or each voter; the players are many and confusing, and though there may be only two major presidential candidates, they always address us through many spokesmen. Moreover, there are concurrent elections at many levels with all sorts of overlap in issues, organizations, and spokesmen. The tradition of behavior, which determines the degree of civility, is weak; indeed the tradition often works the other way (candidates always have attributed malevolence to their opponents). There is no enforcer or judge other than the ultimate election day judgment of

snapping at the heels of his rivals, there is little incentive to develop broadly based programs that differ markedly from the status quo. The voters are most likely to be left with an impression of the candidates' deficiencies. And though a President must have the capacity to learn, which often means changing his mind or his priorities, a candidate will find that changing his mind is treated as prima facie evidence of being devious or indecisive. There are, of course, worse possibilities than a politician being wrong, such as being wrong longer than necessary.

It would be possible to design an election system in which a greater variety of truths were presented, in which there was a greater likelihood that each voter could find a political stance more closely approaching his view of the truth. A multiparty system would be one model. The problem, however, is that under such a system it would be infinitely harder to govern. Also by constitutionally separating the executive and legislative functions of government we have built into the system an adversary incentive. So one trade-off that we have made in choosing a two-party system and the separation of powers doctrine is that we decide elections by an adversary model.

The presidential campaign is an exercise in political arithmetic. The sum sought is 270 electoral votes. The candidates take those actions which they think will attract enough voters to reach their goal. The quintessential political nature of this process allows the country to expect that Presidents will be finely attuned to the decibels of public opinion, that they will operate within the perimeters of acceptability and at a pace best geared to winning support for their proposals, and that

---

the voters, and this comes too late to ensure a high standard of campaign conduct. There is no possibility of compromise or negotiation, for a candidate must either win or lose; and the determinants are not merely facts (even if the facts could be agreed upon) but also personality, emotion, instinct, and other intangibles, all of which have a legitimate place in elections.

they will know how to use the tools of public persuasion and legislative maneuver.

Having succeeded in climbing a political ladder, however, is no guarantee that a President will seek the sorts of political solutions that promote the greatest degree of progress and the least amount of rancor. Because of flukes of circumstance or for other reasons, at least three twentieth-century Presidents have not been instinctive politicians. Taft, at heart, was a judge; Hoover, a technocrat; Nixon, a secretary of state. Eisenhower has often and incorrectly been put in this category because he had never sought elective office and had an aversion to partisan politics. But he was intuitively a brilliant bureaucratic politician. His military experience in World War II had not been as a battlefield warrior but as a political organizer of warriors. Nixon, on the other hand, mistakenly has been grouped among the politician Presidents.

One of the anomalies of Nixon was that he had run for more elective offices than any other twentieth-century President and he hated politics. He had always felt trivialized by the rituals of campaigning. Though he had mastered the political rituals, the lessons of politics were learned rather than felt, and as such they could be quickly unlearned. To repeat, the rituals of the campaign serve a purpose. They force the candidate upon the people and the people upon the candidate. For Nixon, however, politics had been the means to an end. Arriving at the goal, he organized his time and White House staff so as to devote himself largely to foreign policy. To the degree that he overdelegated political concerns, Watergate can be viewed as the end result of a process of presidential disengagement from domestic politics. Ironically, one post-Watergate school of thought now seeks correction in further depoliticizing the system, rather than in restoring the checks and balances of politics.[18] Politicians do not burglarize the

18. One proposal to depoliticize the presidency would limit a President to a single six-year term, thereby eliminating behavior that presumably might be motivated by an incumbent's desire to get reelected. In

opposition (if only because the risks of getting caught are too great); politicians do not wire-tap (if only because too many people would know and someone would talk); politicians do not let their parties atrophy (if only because they will need party leaders in their debt); politicians do not seek solitude as a way of life (if only because it is through wide contacts that they get votes).

Nixon in short was a remarkable exception in a system geared to producing political Presidents. Few other people can be expected to put up with so much that they find unpleasant for so long. As a rule, the system screens out those who find the selection process distasteful. Treasury Secretary Robert Anderson, for example, would not allow Eisenhower to designate him as his chosen successor; he had no desire for a political calling.[19] In an office that must rely on the delicate political antennae of its occupant for effective action, there is real reason to be concerned over proposed changes that might catapult a person without political instinct into the White House.

---

the words of the measure's co-sponsor Senator Mike Mansfield: "It is just intolerable that a President of the United States—any President, whatever his party—is compelled to devote his time, energy, and talents to what can be termed only as purely political tasks. . . . A President under a single, 6-year term would not be removed entirely from politics, but the amount of time he would have to allot to politics would be decreased considerably and by the same token the amount of time he would be able to spend on looking after the national interest, both domestically and in the field of foreign policy, would be increased." Most witnesses at the 1971 hearings on the proposal were in opposition. The general feeling was that a successful President had to be a successful politician and that politics, though perhaps not held in high repute, is an essential part of democracy. A President who is removed from politics will become a President remote from the processes of government and removed from the thoughts and aspirations of his people. See *Single Six-Year Term for President*, Hearings before the Subcommittee on Constitutional Amendments of the Senate Committee on the Judiciary, 92 Cong. 1 sess. (1971), pp. 32, 36, 63, 127.

19. See Herbert S. Parmet, *Eisenhower and the American Crusades* (Macmillan, 1972), pp. 526–27.

No leadership selection process in any other democratic country is as intensely personal as the American political campaign. The parties provide no protection for their presidential candidates, who must live by their wits. The press is persistent in its demands. The people expect to know things about the candidates' private lives to an extent that would be considered impertinent in other societies. By election day the voters have had the opportunity to learn a great deal about the candidates' backgrounds and styles. The question of how well a campaign tests for acceptable presidential style then becomes tautological: a President must have a style that is acceptable to a majority of Americans; if he can get elected, his style is acceptable to a majority of Americans.

No political office (not even Vice President) can prepare a President for being a public person as defined here. Edmund S. Muskie, a senator and former governor, found that being a vice-presidential nominee in 1968 was "an exhilarating experience."[20] But four years later, when seeking the presidency, he discovered that attacks on his wife were more nightmare than exhilaration. The only testing—and training—for this aspect of the presidency is to run for President. The day a candidate acquires his own press corps, and now his own Secret Service detail, is the day acclimatization begins.

Unfortunately, the presidential selection process gives us almost no guidance on whether a candidate has the necessary executive qualities. Candidates do not turn management questions into campaign issues. Management is the structure of governance, not the substance of politics; campaigns are about politics, not governance. Occasionally the argument will be heard that a candidate who knows how to run a campaign must know how to run the country or, conversely, that if a candidate cannot run his own campaign well, he will not be able to run the country. Every now and then a campaign will be so mismanaged as to make this an issue of sorts. But

20. Edmund S. Muskie, *Journeys* (Doubleday, 1972), p. 57.

despite greater press attention to the technical proficiency of campaign management, few voters make the connection.

Moreover, executives are not what people seek in a President. Mencken would write of Herbert Hoover's "reputation as a competent and intelligent administrator—which is precisely the last thing that the endless hordes and herds of the common people ever give a thought to."[21] But Mencken, as was his habit, misread the intuitive wisdom of the "hordes and herds" in correctly ordering priorities. Our Presidents, more often than not, have been atrocious administrators. They often come from an occupation (legislator) and a profession (law) that ill prepares them for management. The parallels between management in the public and private sectors are too tenuous to expect businessmen to perform in a much superior manner. The dilemma of Presidents as executives is more likely to be resolved by refining the job description of the presidency than by changing the selection process. For those who enjoy a little irony with their political science, one might consider that the management structure that contributed to producing Watergate was devised by the most management-conscious President in American history. Perhaps, as Reedy suggests, "the institutionalized approach tends to drive out the political approach."[22]

An acceptable selection process can no more ensure that every President will be acceptable in the performance of his duties than can blood lines always predict that a racehorse will be a champion. But a selection process at least should be designed to test the right qualities. To the degree it is

21. H. L. Mencken, *A Carnival of Buncombe* (Johns Hopkins Press, 1956), p. 11 (reprinted from the *Baltimore Evening Sun*, May 12, 1920). In a similar vein, Alistair Cooke would dismiss Thomas Dewey as "a fine administrator. He was admired by the people who worked for him in the government of New York State; he was respected by the party leaders for his impeccable sense of organization, his forthrightness, his expert calm among the minutiae of government." *Listener* (Sept. 10, 1959), p. 376.

22. See R. Gordon Hoxie (ed.), *The White House: Organization and Operations* (Center for the Study of the Presidency, 1971), p. 167.

found wanting, changes should be proposed. If one system cannot equally test the personal, political, and executive talents that are necessary in the White House, the process should give priority to testing the personal. For they are the most immutable, the least likely to be changed by experience in office. Presidents can become politicians and executives; they are not likely to become better persons.

THREE Availability

☆ ☆ ☆ ☆ ☆ ☆ ☆ ☆ ☆ ☆ ☆ ☆ ☆ ☆ ☆

*Who runs for President? It is perfectly possible
to have a system that works well in probing
the assets and liabilities of those who offer
themselves to the electorate, yet fails to produce
a sufficient pool of talent from which to make
the selection . . .*

SUMMING UP the history of what kinds of
Americans have become presidential candidates, D. W. Brogan wrote in 1954: "Certain rules for availability are fixed.
The candidate must come from a state with a large electoral
vote and from a state that is not certain to vote for the party
candidate. . . . These considerations have ensured that, in
this century, only one candidate has been nominated from a
small state, Mr. Landon of Kansas in 1936. . . . No congressional leader of the very first rank, save James Madison, has
ever been elected President. . . . For in Congress, it is often
necessary to take a line; to choose sides. The leading congressional candidates are almost certain to have angered some
group, injured some interests, to be associated with some legislation or with opposition to some legislation that may, so the
timid fear, cost many, many votes in a presidential election. . . . After the defeat of Governor Smith in 1928 it is
unlikely that a Catholic will be nominated in the foreseeable
future and a *fortiori* a Jew or a Negro is ruled out on the
simple grounds that such a nomination would alienate more
voters than it could possibly gain. . . . There are, of course,
more specific forms of availability than being a male Gentile,

White, Protestant from a large and doubtful state. In this century, there is no doubt what office provides the best springboard for a presidential candidate. It is being or having been (being is much better), Governor of a large, doubtful state, especially the State of New York."[1]

If the Brogan assessment were to be revised today, it would have to note the following post-1954 developments:

Governors. Two elected governors of New York, Averell Harriman and Nelson Rockefeller, have in recent years tried and failed to become presidential nominees. Indeed, no incumbent governor has been nominated since 1952, and Roosevelt in 1932 was the last governor to be elected President.

Small states. Recent presidential nominees have come from Arizona and South Dakota; other contenders for the Democratic nomination in 1972 came from Maine, Oklahoma, Indiana, Iowa, Arkansas, North Carolina, Washington, and Alabama, and none can be considered to have been rejected solely on the basis of their places of residence.

Doubtful states. Since both parties now have carried the electoral vote of every state at some time (except the solidly Democratic District of Columbia), all states can be considered "doubtful" in varying degrees. It probably is more accurate to say that neither party in recent years has been greatly influenced in its nominations by this consideration.

Congressional candidates. All major party nominees since 1960 have served in the Senate, and three out of eight were senators at the time of their nominations; one or both parties undoubtedly will have senators contending for the nominations in 1976.

Minority groups. Not only was a Catholic elected President in 1960, but some have contended that the Democrats would have had their best chance of winning in 1972 if they

1. D. W. Brogan, *Politics in America* (Harper, 1954), pp. 197–200. The same sort of analysis can be found in Malcolm Moos and Stephen Hess, *Hats in the Ring: The Making of Presidential Candidates* (Random House, 1960), esp. Chap. 3.

had nominated a Catholic.[2] A Jew, Senator Abraham Ribi-
coff, was offered the Democratic vice-presidential nomination
in 1972, and a Negro, Senator Edward Brooke, is often men-
tioned for a place on a future Republican ticket.

Brogan might have added that presidential candidates are
usually in their fifties or early sixties. He also could have
pointed out that rarely is a losing nominee given a second
chance, there having been only three modern exceptions
(Cleveland, Bryan, and Dewey) at the time his book was
published. Since then, three nominees have been in their
forties, and two previously defeated candidates have been
given renominations. In an electoral sense, what Kennedy did
for Catholics, Nixon did for losers.

One might conclude that the system has been under great
pressure to change in recent years and that it has proved
highly adaptable. It is a proposition worth examining.

Clearly our latest crop of presidential candidates come
from two institutions, the Senate and the vice presidency.
Governors have declined in availability. All others—Cabinet
officers, members of the House of Representatives, mayors,
non-officeholders—rarely even get into the on-deck circle.

The reasons for the rather abrupt switch from statehouse
to Capitol Hill in producing presidential contenders have
been often stated: the flow of power to Washington, with
vastly expanded budgets, proliferation of grant-in-aid programs, and less obvious but equally centripetal forces, such
as a truly national communications medium; the problems
governors encountered during the 1960s in trying to perform
their duties without incurring serious political bruises, while
the less-exposed legislators did not have to share equally in
governmental failures; the ability of those in the nation's
capital to dominate the news, in part because Washington is
where political-governmental news is written; a lessening of
party control over the nominating process; and the predom-

2. See Louis H. Bean, *How To Predict the 1972 Election* (Quadrangle,
1972), pp. 84–85, 218.

inance of international relations in our lives, the high stakes of war and peace, the heightened role in the world that the United States has assumed for itself since World War II, all of which is outside the purview of leaders in the states.

The senators who successfully aspire to presidential nominations are neither the ordinary legislators, who stick close to constituent problems and keep low profiles, nor, at the other extreme, are they powerful Senate leaders. The record of legislative giants who have caught White House fever is one of total disaster—Champ Clark, Oscar Underwood, John Nance Garner, Alben Barkley, Robert Kerr, Arthur Vandenberg, Robert Taft, William Knowland, Lyndon Johnson (1960), Wilbur Mills. Moreover, when one of this number became president-by-accident, the skills and habits that he brought with him from the Senate were not an unalloyed blessing. Lyndon Johnson did get a massive program through the Congress in 1964–65 in sharp contrast to his predecessor (who had not been a Senate leader), but the traits of the cloakroom often worked against Johnson and made him suspect in the eyes of the public and the press. A President cannot afford to appear too devious in manner or ingenious in device. There is a difference between legislative intrigue and presidential intrigue; Franklin Roosevelt was a genius at the latter and failed notably when he attempted the former. Leadership in the closed society of the Senate, with its accepted traditions of bargaining, "creative compromise," and petty favors, when transferred to the presidency can create a dangerous mind-set, an attitude of "every man has his price." On the other hand, the legislators who do get presidential nominations usually have not subscribed to "the folkways" of the Senate: long apprenticeships, dull legislative spadework, unhurried deliberation, heavy specialization.[3] Rather, they are what their colleagues scornfully call "show horses" or "grandstanders."

3. See Donald R. Matthews, *U.S. Senators and Their World* (University of North Carolina Press, 1960), esp. Chap. 5.

The emergence of the vice presidency from Throttlebottom to heir-apparent was largely brought about by Dwight Eisenhower's distaste for partisan politicking and the way that aversion coincided with the fortuitous circumstance of having the oldest President in history coupled with the second youngest Vice President. Presidents had given special assignments to their Vice Presidents since Franklin Roosevelt, and an increased awareness of the importance of preparing the Vice President resulted from Truman's sudden assumption of the presidential office. But no President before Eisenhower gave his Vice President as many chores or as much exposure.

Turning the Vice President into an instant celebrity and a chief party spokesman, both at the same time, guaranteed that he would have a leg up on the next available presidential nomination. (It also places him in an extremely difficult position from which to win elections.)[4]

The enlargement of vice-presidential duties is not without grave risks. The writers of the Constitution had reasons for creating (in John Adams' words) "the most insignificant office that ever the invention of man contrived." Nixon, looking back on his years as Vice President, once wrote that a President ran "the risk of turning him [the Vice President] into merely another bureaucrat—and a 'Secretary of Catch-All Affairs' at that!"[5] A Vice President cannot be treated as a bureaucrat, even one of Cabinet rank. For it may be in the public interest for a President to "sacrifice" any public official

4. Writing of Vice President Humphrey's race for the presidency in 1968, Edmund Muskie said that he "had none of the advantages that an incumbent President usually enjoys. . . . He was seeking ways to make himself an independent candidate, to be his own man, without being disloyal [to Johnson]." *Journeys* (Doubleday, 1972), p. 54. This was also the dilemma faced by Nelson W. Polsby when writing a pro-Humphrey tract: "It would not be correct to say that he [Humphrey] has been important in the making of Vietnam policy." *The Citizen's Choice, Humphrey or Nixon* (Public Affairs Press, 1968), p. 35.

5. Richard M. Nixon, "The Second Office," *The 1964 World Book Year Book* (Field Enterprises, 1964), pp. 93–94.

of his creation, as Eisenhower did in the case of Sherman Adams, and he should not put himself in a position where that public official may be the Vice President, his constitutionally anointed successor in the event of death or incapacitation. Presidential leadership requires that a President must hold accountable his appointees. If they fail, they can be disgraced and removed. But a Vice President is different: he cannot be removed by the President; he should not be disgraced. So the only responsibilities that a President should give to his Vice President are bureaucratically marginal or symbolic. That the trend is otherwise is to be regretted. Some have argued that a job without major responsibilities cannot attract good people and that a President should even consider appointing the Vice President to one of the major Cabinet departments.[6] Though it is true that some men have declined vice-presidential nominations in recent years, there is no evidence that they did so because of the nature of the office or that there were not enough other good candidates willing to make the race. Eugene McCarthy gave the proper job description when he wrote: "A Vice President in office should be treated much as a crown prince is treated in a monarchy. He should be trained in the arts of government. He should not be used in the temporary and transient affairs of state. He should be protected from partisan strife."[7]

The reasons for choosing a vice-presidential candidate, a prerogative of the presidential nominee, generally have little to do with qualifications for assuming the presidency. The ticket balancing may be ideological (Wendell Willkie-Charles McNary, 1940), geographical (John Kennedy-Lyndon Johnson, 1960), religious (three of the last four Democratic pairings have been Catholic-Protestant or vice versa), part of a deal to assure the presidential nomination (Frank-

6. See Donald E. Graham, "The Vice Presidency: What It Is, What It Could Be," *Washington Post*, Sept. 18, 1972.

7. Eugene J. McCarthy, "The Crown Prince," *New York Times*, Aug. 17, 1972.

lin Roosevelt-John Nance Garner, 1932), or even to detract least from the ticket. (The *New York Times* contended, "Responding to the message of those polls [which showed that Nixon in 1968 would run less well with a prominent partner, such as Reagan or Hatfield, than he would by himself], Mr. Nixon chose Mr. Agnew because he was the closest he could come to a political cipher."[8]) A profile of vice-presidential nominees looks somewhat different from that of presidential nominees. The candidates for Vice President are most apt to have a background of holding high appointive office (Henry Wallace and Sargent Shriver) rather than elective office; of coming from outside the political ranks (Frank Knox, publishing); or of being younger, less experienced legislators and governors (Nixon, Eagleton, Agnew). Thus, although often picked for the "wrong" reasons, the new prominence of Vice Presidents has had the effect of broadening the talent pool from which Presidents are eventually drawn.

The change in emphasis from governors to senators and Vice Presidents as an example of the system's adaptability may be more apparent than real. Although the Senate has been called a vocational school for Presidents, in fact serving in the Senate confers no special presidential skills except possibly the habit of taking a national point of view. What the Senate has given aspirants is a grand platform from which to launch a campaign for the White House. The real change that has come about through turning more often to senators is to erase the discrimination of geography, to equalize the ability of political leaders from all states—small as well as large—to seek the presidency. Although Vice Presidents, with their collection of minor bureaucratic duties, acquire no special presidential skills, they do have the opportunity to observe a President in action from close range.

The problem, of course, is to identify that background

8. "Intact Team" (editorial), *New York Times*, Aug. 24, 1972.

which is most likely to produce a skillful President. It might be helpful for a President to have been both senator and governor (22 percent of the senators during the period 1947–57 fitted this description).[9] However, if a person is doubly qualified in this way, he may be too old to meet effectively the demands of the office. A successful formula might be a U.S. senator with Cabinet experience, say as secretary of state. This would have made James Buchanan the ideal candidate for President. The least qualified elected President would have been Lincoln (one term in the House of Representatives, defeated for the Senate). Theodore Roosevelt in explaining his stewardship theory chose Lincoln and Buchanan to illustrate the right and wrong ways to be President.

It is not surprising that television has figured prominently in the fates of modern candidates—Kefauver's televised Senate committee hearings on organized crime in 1950, Nixon's "Checkers speech," the 1960 debates, Muskie's speech on the eve of the 1970 congressional elections, which propelled him into the front-runner slot for the Democratic presidential nomination. But Lincoln's fortunes were equally affected by a "debate," Charles Evans Hughes' by an "investigation," and Bryan's by a "speech." So one concludes that candidates employ—successfully or not—the tools of communications at hand. The startling fact is that there is no recognizable difference in the types of people who run for President in the TV era and those who ran in earlier times. Much has been said about "charisma"; yet a simple listing of nominees since 1952 disproves the notion that "good looks," voice, or other properties have changed much in the scale by which we measure electability. The speaking styles and abilities of Dwight Eisenhower and John Kennedy were of different orders of elegance. Barry Goldwater is a handsome man, as was Warren G. Harding; Lyndon Johnson is not thought of in this class, and neither was Woodrow Wilson. Perhaps as Garry Wills writes

9. Matthews, U.S. Senators and Their World, p. 55.

of Nixon, "[P]eople vote for him despite his appearance."[10] Nor, indeed, has TV altered the nature of the issues in presidential campaigns. Only two noteworthy changes in the selection process can be attributed in a direct sense to television. The first is that "favorite sons" are no longer a regular feature at the conventions, TV exposure being too valuable to risk boring potential voters. (This development narrows the talent pool, though not seriously.) Second, and more important, is the turn toward federal officeholders (and away from those in the states) as most likely to succeed in the presidential sweepstakes.

Television will remain the one constant among those factors that tend to disadvantage the governors as a class; all others are subject to change, and change which may come sooner than many have forecast. If the electorate swings toward isolationism, this will add to the attractiveness of politicians who have been dealing with domestic concerns. Then, too, ambitious governors will try to compensate for their lack of involvement in international relations by embarking on fact-finding trips abroad, foreign trade missions, and other overseas assignments. The size of future revenue-sharing packages could well make the governors' records more appealing, especially if, at the same time, federal deficits continue to mount. Changes in party rules, such as those initiated by the Democrats after 1968, could move the base of nominating power back into the local communities. And in a universe as small as presidential nominations, it does not take many dynamic (and lucky) governors to revise the conventional wisdom. Although it is premature to write the obituary of governors as presidential possibilities, this does not assume that all governors are equal. If TV has removed the shackles from senators representing small states, among governors it may work in favor of those from large states, particularly New York, California, and Illinois, where (in addition to Washington, D.C.) the networks base most of their camera crews and correspondents.

10. Garry Wills, *Nixon Agonistes* (Signet Books, 1970), p. 29.

The main point is that even though the *backgrounds* of potential Presidents have changed in recent years, the system continues to produce the same *types* of people. Whether senators, governors, or Vice Presidents, those who become major party nominees are *professional politicians*. What they all have in common is that they have run for office successfully. This is no modest distinction when trying to separate those with personal presidential qualities (the ability to communicate, stamina, style, openness) and political presidential qualities (flexibility, sensitivity, an instinct for public opinion) from other professionals whose assets are judged by different standards. The system generally excludes the *non-politician*. Like all professional selection systems, this one demands an apprenticeship, a pretesting. It is not realistic to expect anyone to start at the top of a profession (except in a hereditary system), and the presidency is the top of the political profession. The only other occupational avenue to the presidency on any scale has been the military, also a public profession but not one credited with producing many notable Presidents.

The system however, is not entirely closed—the most exceptional outsider having been Wendell Willkie, the businessman who won the 1940 Republican nomination. As early as 1937 a columnist in the Worcester, Massachusetts, *Telegram* suggested that Willkie would make a good candidate; eventually other columnists, such as Arthur Krock of the *New York Times* and Raymond Moley in *Newsweek*, began referring to him as a possible nominee. Willkie made impressive guest appearances on popular radio shows ("America's Town Meeting of the Air" and "Information Please"); his writings turned up in major magazines (*Fortune, Reader's Digest, Atlantic Monthly*); he addressed such influential groups as the American Newspaper Publishers Association.[11] Even then Willkie's nomination was possible only because of circumstances over which he had no control. In terms of his own behavior, how-

11. See Herbert S. Parmet and Marie B. Hecht, *Never Again: A President Runs for a Third Term* (Macmillan, 1968), pp. 62, 70, 84, 88, 90, 91.

ever, Willkie was acting as a politician, and his success attested to his professionalism.

There also is a "two-step" process for bringing nonprofessionals into presidential contention. George Romney, Charles Percy, and Ronald Reagan are recent examples of men who achieved status outside the political arena and then turned to elective politics in their middle years. Even though these three happened to reside in large swing states, their instant recognition by the press as potential Presidents was more a result of the celebrity qualities they brought with them to office. That Romney, Percy, and Reagan are Republicans may be coincidental (although the minority party has greater need to look outside its political ranks for talent), but it is clear that their career pattern runs counter to the traditional ladder to the presidency, which is to start early in elective politics. It has been a rule of thumb that a nonmilitary person does not get to be President unless he has run for something before the age of thirty.

One way to give different types of people a chance to become nominees is to change the makeup of the group doing the selecting. The Democratic rules changes in 1972, governing the proportion of convention delegates that must be women, members of minority groups, and youth, can be viewed as such an attempt. That the nominee chosen was then soundly defeated may send the party chieftains back to the drawing board, but the proposition that different types of delegates may choose different types of candidates now has a basis in fact. A second way of procuring different types of nominees is to change the process by which they are selected. The alternative generally proposed is the direct national primary.[12] But this would narrow the pool of talent by giving an advantage to the candidate who raised the greatest amount of money. (The present system of seriatim state primaries,

12. The best-known proposal for a direct national primary was introduced in the form of a proposed constitutional amendment by Senators Mike Mansfield and George Aiken on March 13, 1972. The Mansfield-Aiken plan calls for a primary in early August; if no candidate won at

which accidentally progresses from smaller to larger states, allows a candidate to enter the field with relatively little start-up money.)[13] The national primary is opposed by those of us who believe that the two-party system should be strengthened. In practice, it is imaginable that the national primary would move the United States toward a no-party system: through court challenges or individual preferences, it would enfranchise more and more people who have less and less attachment to party—either "free riders" (who temporarily adopt a party label in order to vote for a particular candidate without serious commitment to that party) or "trouble makers" (whose aim is other than to give a party the strongest candidate possible), as sometimes happens in states with crossover primaries.[14] A third way to broaden the talent pool is through a multiparty system—increase the number of candidates by increasing the number of parties. A fourth way could be called the shotgun approach, which would attempt to propel more candidates into the present system. One method might be to superimpose over the convention structure a series of recommending conferences to be held at the beginning of the presidential election year. Groups designated by the parties' national committees—such as the Democratic and Republican Governors Conferences, the Democratic and

---

least 40 percent of the vote, a run-off election would be held twenty-eight days later. Candidates would qualify for the primary by filing petitions signed by a certain percentage of voters nationwide. The purpose of the conventions would be to write the platforms and pick the vice-presidential nominees.

13. William R. Keech, "Presidential Nominating Politics: Problems of Popular Choice" (paper delivered at the 1972 annual meeting of the American Political Science Association).

14. Whereas Gallup polls for many years have reflected popular support for national primaries, most political scientists who specialize in American politics have been opposed. See Paul T. David, Ralph M. Goldman, and Richard C. Bain, *The Politics of National Party Conventions* (Brookings Institution, 1960), pp. 489–90; Malcolm Moos, "New Light on the Nominating Process," in *Research Frontiers in Politics and Government* (Brookings Institution, 1955), pp. 157–58, 163; Gerald Pomper, *Nominating the President* (Norton Library, 1966), pp. 216–30.

Republican Mayors Conferences, and the Democratic and Republican Congressional Caucuses—could propose a candidate whose name automatically would be placed in nomination at the conventions. Candidates also could be nominated by national petition (with a substantial number of signatures required). Neither method should carry with it any convention votes. They would be designed simply to encourage additional candidates to seek the nomination.

Not all political scientists agree that we would be better off with a larger number of presidential possibilities. Donald Matthews argues that increasing the number would "probably not" be an improvement. He contends: "The difficulties of arriving at a decentralized collective choice in a reasonably democratic way are rapidly compounded as the number of alternatives increases. Our present nominating procedures were severely strained, for example, by the unusually large number of fairly evenly matched candidates the Democrats had this year [1972]. It is hard to imagine the chaos that might have ensued if there had been two or three times more!"[15] My view is that the candidates in 1972 fell by the wayside quite naturally (sometimes even gracefully) and that the system was not strained by the temporary presence of John Lindsay, Sam Yorty, Harold Hughes, Fred Harris, or Birch Bayh. (What may be strained by a plethora of candidates, however, is the capacity of the press on which we rely for our political information.) Non-politicians—business executives, union leaders, academics, and so forth—should be encouraged to seek the presidency, but they should be tested through an essentially political process. If, as I believe, professional politicians are more likely to possess presidential qualities, then the present system can accomplish this end, although appropriate adjustments and a method for equalizing financial resources among candidates should be adopted to give the electorate a wider range of possibilities.

15. Donald R. Matthews, "The Emergence of Presidential Candidates" (paper delivered at the 1972 annual meeting of the American Political Science Association).

FOUR

Functions of the Campaign

☆ ☆ ☆ ☆ ☆ ☆ ☆ ☆ ☆ ☆ ☆ ☆ ☆ ☆ ☆

> The campaign is primarily a process of personnel
> selection. But it is more than the electorate
> operating as a gigantic search committee. The
> campaign also serves as corrective, the righting
> of perceived wrongs; as policy formulation, the
> proposal and approval of issue positions; as
> national self-examination, and as entertain-
> ment . . .

IF JUST ONE WORD could be used to describe
the nine-month presidential contest from the New Hampshire
primary through Election Day, the word would have to be
"ordeal." By evolution rather than design we have constructed
an elaborate obstacle course for our potential Presidents: tor-
tuous, winding, fatiguing, and cruel; requiring the building of
staff, the delegation of responsibilities, the allocation of resources, the planning of strategy, the selection of positions,
the making of instant decisions, the use of rhetoric, the ability
to function under pressure, to take criticism and keep coming
back, to time and coordinate events, and not to lose touch
with the people somewhere along the way.

In late 1967, George Romney, then frontrunner for the
Republican nomination, told a Detroit television interviewer
that he had experienced "the greatest brainwashing that anybody can get when you go over to Vietnam." Romney's poll
rating immediately dropped from 24 to 14 points, and he

withdrew from the race before the first primary was held.[1] In 1972, while campaigning in the New Hampshire primary, Edmund Muskie, then frontrunner for the Democratic nomination, "broke down in uncontrollable tears that were captured by TV cameras" when replying to a newspaper story about his wife.[2] Muskie's New Hampshire vote was disappointing and in April he withdrew from contesting primaries. To say that Romney's "brainwashing" or Muskie's "tears" were the reasons for their failures would be misleading; yet these events became the symbols of their weaknesses in the public mind, weaknesses that became apparent only as a result of the ordeal. The manner in which some are eliminated may border on the brutal, but running for public office is not an obligatory activity in our society.

The Campaign as Personnel Selection

Our problem as voters is that we must choose a President for the future; though we may make our judgment on the basis of the past, whoever we elect will have to serve us for the *next* four years, years in which the most crucial decisions may well be about matters that are currently unknown. "It would be great if they handed you a check list of problems, and after you were elected you could go down the list bing-bing-bing and take care of all the problems," said Kevin White. "But that's not what happens. I had no way of knowing that two months after I took office as mayor of Boston [in 1967], that the biggest problem I would face would be getting fuel oil into the city to keep the people warm. That's not the kind of thing you can anticipate. What you need in office is a man who can cope with situations as they arise,

1. See Theodore H. White, *The Making of the President 1968* (Pocket Books, 1970), pp. 71–73, and Louis H. Bean, *How To Predict the 1972 Election* (Quadrangle, 1972), p. 148.
2. Myra MacPherson, "Jane Muskie: A Wife Becomes 'an Issue,'" *Washington Post*, March 12, 1972.

situations that no one even thought of."[3] Circumstances change, crises arise, one cannot know the unknowable, and our dilemma becomes how can we judge without certified knowledge. What would a potential President do if the Soviet Union put offensive missiles in Cuba, or if unemployment and inflation rose at the same time, or if North Korea invaded South Korea, or if the East Germans built a wall between East and West Berlin?

So in place of a bing-bing-bing checklist we insist that our potential Presidents run an obstacle course. A candidate, as in 1972, suddenly discovers that his running-mate has a record of serious mental illness; a candidate, as in 1952, suddenly discovers that his running-mate has a "secret" fund of $18,000 contributed by wealthy supporters. The candidates must make a decision, quickly, in full public view. Will they retain a vice-presidential nominee or will they replace the person? And in watching the candidates in the act of making decisions we are given the opportunity to learn something about them, something that is useful in trying to assess how they might respond to sudden crisis if they were in the White House.

Complaints have been heard in recent years, especially in 1972, that the presidential selection process takes far too long. The origins of this criticism become clearer when we recall some recent history: two of the last three elections, 1964 and 1972, were landslide victories; 1968 was a contest between two durable politicians who had been on the national scene for a generation. Campaigns of predictable outcome or lacking excitement *seem* longer. They also may seem longer because television more quickly sates whatever public appetite there is for political fare. And the refinement of public opinion surveys has made them more predictable. Campaigns, in fact, are not getting longer. It probably always has been true that

3. Quoted in Joseph Napolitan, *The Election Game* (Doubleday, 1972), p. 129.

the candidates for President begin in earnest immediately after the preceding midterm election.[4]

Two reasons often are given as to why presidential campaigns should be shortened. First, the technology now exists to inform the electorate quickly, and, second, the long campaign is said to bore the electorate, thereby lowering the voter turnout.[5] Yet the lowest voter turnout of the modern era (52 percent in 1948) came in an exciting and unpredictable four-way race for President, and there are controversial explanations for the 55 percent turnout in 1972.[6] On the other hand,

4. Andrew Jackson was "nominated" for President by the Tennessee legislature three years before the 1828 election. On July 5, 1927, H. L. Mencken wrote in the *Baltimore Evening Sun*, "The chief danger confronting the Al Smith boom lies in the fact that it started too soon." Smith, of course, won the 1928 Democratic nomination. James Farley spent two years before the 1932 convention rounding up delegates for Roosevelt. John Kennedy's drive for the 1960 nomination began in 1956 and has been called "the campaign-before-the-campaign." George McGovern announced his candidacy twenty-two months before the election of 1972.

5. President Eisenhower argued that campaigns consist of "fairly fruitless words" and could be shortened to thirty days "without changing the result decisively." See Eisenhower, *Waging Peace* (Doubleday, 1965), p. 18. Eisenhower was right in that only in very close elections, such as in 1960, will enough voters make up or change their minds during the "official" campaign (Labor Day through Election Day) to actually affect the results. For example, the voters had agreed to reelect Nixon in 1972 *before* the Democrats even nominated a candidate, according to both Daniel Yankelovich and Louis Harris. See "Why Nixon Won," *New York Review of Books* (Nov. 30, 1972), p. 7, and speech by Louis Harris, National Press Club, Washington, D.C., Nov. 10, 1972. But, of course, a presidential selection system cannot be based on the assumption that every election will be a landslide. Half the presidential elections in this century have not been landslides.

6. Seymour Martin Lipset and Earl Raab consider the low voter turnout in 1972 as "an expression not so much of apathy as of liberal-conservative ambivalence." See "The Election and the National Mood," *Commentary*, Vol. 55 (January 1973), p. 48. Walter Dean Burnham, in an unpublished "pre-mortem" of the 1972 election, views poor levels of voting participation as part of "a deep-seated crisis in belief system and underlying social structure." Richard Scammon thinks some of the 1972 vote falloff was caused by the enfranchisement of eighteen-to-twenty-year-

no evidence shows that a low turnout is a product of bore-dom and a long campaign. Moreover, though television pro-vides the means of informing voters quickly, all voters do not tune into politics at the same time. Those who are least in-formed politically are also the least educated and poorest.[7] An election system in a democratic society must allow for its "least informed members" to have the opportunity to catch up. It is, however, the "best informed" who most appear to have lost patience with the long process which results in the election of a President. At the same time, the steady disinte-gration of political party identification, a factor that once accounted for 60 percent of voter preference in presidential elections, may mean that more people now will be relying on events during the campaign to help them decide.

Viewed from the perspective of the candidates, the long campaign also serves as an equalizer. When an incumbent is running, which has been two-thirds of the time in this century, rarely will the out-party candidate be as well known. A first-term President is running for reelection every day he is in office; the challenger needs a campaign to make front-page headlines on a regular basis. He needs added time to transmit his ideas and his personality to the electorate. He needs added time to build an organization. In short, the long campaign can benefit the underdog.

A short campaign would be easier to manipulate—candi-dates would have to put greater emphasis on televised cam-paigning; fewer people would have the opportunity to see the candidates in person; it would be more difficult to separate the "real" candidates from the creations of their ghostwriters and public relations specialists.

---

olds, young people traditionally voting at a lower rate than their elders. Richard Smolka believes that people are now less likely to feel that their problems can be solved at the ballot box. See William Chapman, "The Vanishing Voter," *Washington Post*, Jan. 28, 1973.

7. See Angus Campbell and others, *Elections and the Political Order* (Wiley, 1966), p. 136.

Shortening the campaign, even if desirable, is far easier to propose than to accomplish. Moving the primaries closer to the conventions or moving the conventions closer to Election Day, the suggestions most often put forth, might shorten the homestretch but not the track. The presidency seekers still would begin their active quests when it best served their interests. (And recent experience is that the earlier a candidate gets started, the better his chances.) Probably the only effective way to shorten the campaign would be to abolish the fixed-term presidency, replacing it with something along the lines of the British model in which the head of government has the right to call a new election at any time within a given period. Such a system would entail additional expenses, assuming that other contests were not brought into conformity; create possible problems of overheating the political system by increasing the number of elections; and, in a nonparliamentary form of government, give a decided advantage to the incumbent, who would choose an election date that maximized his chances.

The result desired by opponents of the long campaign might be achieved, not by shortening the number of days, but by limiting the number or timing of candidates' activities. This is a variant of whether a tree falling in the forest makes a noise if no one is around to hear it fall. Does a campaign exist if the candidates are prevented from advertising themselves? One proposal calls for a five-week limit on campaign advertising.[8] Rules of this sort could be challenged in the courts as violations of free speech. The best chance of skirting the constitutional question might be to tie formal limits into optional public financing: a candidate who accepted public financing of his campaign would have to agree to certain conditions, including a time-frame in which the money would be spent.

But shortening the campaign is not desirable. It is exactly

8. See Bill Brock, "The Money Problem," *New York Times*, May 14, 1973.

because the campaign is both long and arduous that it eventually penetrates into the field of vision of many Americans; the longer a candidate participates in the ordeal, the greater is the likelihood that his character and instincts will be perceived by the electorate. What Americans have constructed, mostly by accident, is a partial *simulation of the presidency.* In the absence of certainty, this becomes a tool of considerable utility. This simulation operates most effectively when there are hotly contested struggles, which is almost always the case in the out-party or when an incumbent is not seeking reelection. Occasionally, however, this will not happen, as in 1968 when Nixon had a relatively easy nomination fight and then relied on divisiveness among the Democrats to carry him to victory. Also, of course, the simulation is not a necessary factor in judging the presidential qualities of an incumbent. Nixon was criticized in 1972 for failing to campaign, but it is doubtful whether the voters needed further evidence of his capacity to perform the duties of the office; in such instances, the value of the campaign is as corrective.

The Campaign as Corrective

In anticipating the 1968 election, Aaron Wildavsky wrote, "To manifest their displeasure, people will take the Democratic Party, which is in, and throw it out, and take the Republican Party, which is out, and put it in. This instinctive and convulsive changing of the guard need not be caused by a popular belief that the candidate or leaders of one party are better than another. All that is necessary is widespread dissatisfaction and a consequent desire to give a new team a chance."[9] Wildavsky's prediction reflects the most elemental aspect of our system. For in this regard an election is a blunt yet efficient instrument, with the recourse for unacceptable policies being to "throw the rascals out." Most elections are

9. Aaron Wildavsky, *The Presidency* (Little, Brown, 1969), p. 366 (reprinted from *Trans-Action* [October 1968]), p. 8.

retrospective sanctionings, decided more on the basis of the voters' feelings of what has been done to them in the past than on their expectations of what will be done for them in the future. Thus elections have a special appropriateness when an incumbent is running. But an incumbent's party is always running: Adlai Stevenson in 1952 could no more successfully dissociate himself from the Truman administration, although he did not serve in it, than could Vice President Nixon run away from the Eisenhower record in 1960. Though there is a variety of ways in which politicians can be held accountable, from impeachment through legislative votes, elections provide the most regularized system of accountability.

Yet a blunt instrument is not necessarily a just tool. A President is blamed (or tries to take credit) for everything that happens during his tenure, whether he is rightly responsible or not. Still, there is a certain raw logic for periodically giving "a new team a chance" regardless of ideology or even a record of past successes. "I always thought my mind would develop in a high position," Henry Kissinger said in 1972. "But, fatigue becomes a factor. The mind is always working so hard that you learn little. Instead, you tend to work with what you learned in previous years."[10] There are other reasons why an administration loses effectiveness as it ages. Lyndon Johnson, that master of congressional relations, explained to an aide why he could expect problems with Capitol Hill if he sought and won a second term. "Congress always gives a new man a little cooperation, a little breathing room. I'd be the same old Johnson coming back to the well again, beggin' and pushin' 'em to give me a better bill than last year. No. Congress and I are like an old man and woman who've lived together for a hundred years. We know each other's faults and what little good there is in us. We're tired of each

10. Quoted in Norman Mailer, St. George and the Godfather (New American Library, 1972), p. 120.

other."[11] Leo Rosten explained in 1937 why Franklin Roosevelt, that master of press relations, would encounter difficulties in time: "The [press] corps had greeted Mr. Roosevelt with frenzy in 1933; in it there was a will-to-believe which, because it ignored future possibilities and past experience, would end by tearing down the myth it was creating."[12] A President gets tired; it becomes harder for him to attract top-level executives to government service; personality and ideological conflicts develop within an administration; interest groups learn to oppose a President more effectively; the mystique wears off and people get bored; power starts to drift away if a President cannot or will not run for reelection. For such reasons a presidential administration resembles an hourglass—with the sand running down. Elections correct this too.

The Campaign as Policy Formulation

In preparing to seek his party's presidential nomination in 1972, Edmund Muskie wrote that a candidate "must actually develop proposals, policies, and programs to deal with current issues, as far as one can anticipate. That is part of what a campaign is all about."[13] It is also the part of the campaign that is most faulted. Theodore White's dismissal of "the reasonable discussion of issues" as "the dream of unblooded political scientists"[14] has not stopped the flow of criticism against the way candidates and parties spell out what they would do if elected.

It is charged that politicians ignore most issues and break their pledges on those they cannot ignore; that the candidates' speeches are exercises in oversimplification, overdrama-

11. Quoted in Harry McPherson, A Political Education (Little, Brown, 1972), p. 428.

12. Leo C. Rosten, "President Roosevelt and the Washington Correspondents," Public Opinion Quarterly (January 1937), p. 49.

13. Edmund S. Muskie, Journeys (Doubleday, 1972), pp. 50–51.

14. Theodore H. White, The Making of the President 1960 (Pocket Books, 1961), p. 351.

tization, and (if made by the challengers) "overcatastrophiza-tion." The 1932 Democratic platform pledged a balanced budget, and the 1968 Republican platform opposed recognition of Communist China. Roosevelt unbalanced the budget, and Nixon set up an office in Peking. "I do not see a reasonable prospect that I will recommend a guaranteed annual income," Nixon said in the 1968 campaign.[15] Fifteen months later as President he recommended the Family Assistance Plan, a form of guaranteed income for the poor.

The assumption is that such conduct is wrong: that campaigns should be instruments of some precision and intellectual rigor and that candidates should keep their word. After all, our system must ultimately depend on our faith in words.

The overlooked fact is that candidates prefer to keep their word, other things being equal. There are a variety of ways to view Roosevelt's pledge to balance the budget without assuming that he tried to mislead the voters.[16] (1) He thought of it as a long-range goal, which he tried to honor by appointing some fiscal conservatives to key posts, such as Budget Director Lewis Douglas, by cutting federal spending when he thought the time was right, as in 1936–37, and by continuing to pledge a balanced budget in the 1936 platform. (2) In weighing competing demands, he concluded that lowering unemployment deserved a higher priority than balancing the budget. (3) His thinking changed as he was influenced by different economists. Usually some such reasons determine why a President does not honor a pledge: he tries and fails (Nixon resorting to wage-price controls); circumstances change (Eisenhower's containment position and the Hungarian uprising); he learns something he did not know (Kennedy and the "missile gap"). Rarely does a politician gain, at least in the short run, from changing his mind. Even

15. Quoted in Daniel P. Moynihan, *The Politics of a Guaranteed Income* (Random House, 1973), p. 183.
16. See James MacGregor Burns, *Roosevelt: The Lion and the Fox* (Harvest Books, 1956), pp. 167, 171–72, 333.

if one wishes to believe that a candidate's promises are not made in good faith, one must recognize that he is alert to the inherent problems of his acting otherwise. Thus as a rule of thumb and survival, any politician would rather keep his commitments.

But, above all, candidates seek to get elected.[17] In accepting the 1860 Republican nomination, Lincoln asked his supporters to "kindly let me be silent."[18] FDR, after opposing U.S. participation in the League of Nations in 1932, wrote a distressed supporter, "[F]or heaven's sake have a little faith."[19] Issues often are badly handled by candidates because they view winning office, not issue referenda, as the primary outcome of elections; because they contend for office through an adversary system that treats issues as a political football, the vehicle for scoring points; because they contend for office within a framework of two major parties with electoral incentives for blurring disagreements; and because they respond to an electorate that at times is neither knowledgeable about issues nor highly politicized. The issue-ignorance of Americans probably is the most thoroughly documented tenet of voting research. The University of Michigan's Institute for Social Research found that 28 percent of those interviewed in 1964 did not know that there was a Communist regime in China; a majority (three out of five) of those who voted for Eugene McCarthy in the 1968 New Hampshire primary prob-

17. Occasionally there are major-party candidates who do not see the purpose of the campaign as the winning of office. Their purpose is to *educate* the voters. Barry Goldwater was one such candidate, according to his speechwriter. See Karl Hess, *In a Cause That Will Triumph: The Goldwater Campaign and the Future of Conservatism* (Doubleday, 1967), pp. 135, 157. Eugene McCarthy also claimed that his campaign "was essentially an educational one." See his *The Year of the People* (Doubleday, 1969), pp. 84, 106, 316–17. And, of course, "education" is almost always the purpose of minor-party and third-party candidates.

18. Quoted in Bruce Catton, *The Coming Fury* (Doubleday, 1961), p. 91.

19. Quoted in Louis W. Koenig, *The Chief Executive* (Harcourt, Brace and World, 1964), p. 39.

ably did not know that he was a "dove," since they viewed the Johnson administration as not taking a hard enough line in Vietnam![20] For most people the business of earning a living and raising a family is sufficiently difficult, time-consuming, and interesting; running governments usually is left to those with unusual ambitions or leisure.[21] In contrast, those who most criticize campaigns for their absence of reasonable policy debate are typically the most politicized; and having a consuming interest in the affairs of government (without realizing how this sets them apart), they believe that their fellow citizens should have the same passionate concerns.

Viewing policy formulation as a campaign function within this context, it is perhaps remarkable that issues play as large a part as they do or that voters are exposed to as much disagreement or as many precise policy commitments as they are. Though some questions (such as radical alternatives to capitalism) are taboo for the dominant parties, most major economic and social issues have been fought over at some time in some presidential campaign. This is not to say that new policy initiatives are likely to come out of the campaign. This rarely happens, and those that have emerged generally have been modest. The issues in a campaign, by and large, are those that are already in the public arena. But besides focusing attention on existing areas of controversy, a campaign also can reflect areas of consensus. This often leads to complaints that voters are given little choice. Yet Tweedledum-Tweedledee elections generally mirror popular agreement on the aims of society and an acceptable pace of change. In times of polarization, as in 1860, 1896, or the 1930s, the political process produces clear-cut alternatives. The Univer-

20. See Philip E. Converse and others, "Continuity and Change in American Politics: Parties and Issues in the 1968 Election," *American Political Science Review*, Vol. 63 (December 1969), p. 1092.

21. See Peter L. Berger and Richard J. Neuhaus, *Movement and Revolution* (Anchor Books, 1970), p. 16.

sity of Michigan Center for Political Studies notes a trend toward a greater emphasis on issues in presidential politics since the 1960s, with the outcome in 1972 largely determined by the issues, rather than by candidate personality or party loyalty.[22] This could indicate that we are entering another period of polarization.

The development of issues in a presidential campaign often grows out of an intricate interaction between candidate and electorate. Despite the ability of candidates to make their appeals without stepping outside a television studio—and reach more people in the process—they persist in taking their case personally to the voters. This is not what most observers expected to happen once TV became a dominant force in communications. Why candidates have not given up on the jet-age version of the whistlestop, with its high cost in relation to the number of people reached, is an interesting speculation. Certainly many of them must have been advised to do so. The answer may be no more complicated than that the sorts of persons who run for President find that "rubbing shoulders with the people" fills some special need. As Muskie has said, "You get that important response directly from audiences. . . . I read faces in the crowd. Sounds are less significant, although silence is significant. But above all is a feeling in the air."[23] A presidential candidate on the campaign trail is engaged in a process of pulse-taking, seeking the voters' tolerance level, saying the same things over and over again, gauging reactions, dropping ideas, adding others, sharpening lines until the traveling press corps is able to chant them in unison. An example of this exercise, although not in a campaign contest, is recounted by Schlesinger in discussing President Kennedy's tour of the western states in September 1963:

He conscientiously pursued the conservation theme for several

22. Arthur H. Miller and others, "A Majority Party in Disarray: Policy Polarization in the 1972 Election" (paper delivered at the 1973 annual meeting of the American Political Science Association).

23. Muskie, Journeys, p. 61.

speeches. Then late on the second day, at Billings, Montana, he struck, almost by accident, a new note. Mike Mansfield was present, and in his third sentence Kennedy praised the Senate leader for his part in bringing about test ban ratification. To his surprise this allusion produced strong and sustained applause. Heartened, he set forth his hope of lessening the "chance of a military collision between those two great nuclear powers which together have the power to kill 300 million people in the short space of a day." The Billings response encouraged him to make the pursuit of peace increasingly the theme of his trip.[24]

Kennedy went out to talk to westerners about conservation, a subject that *he* thought was uppermost in *their* minds, and discovered that they were more concerned with peace. This was valuable information for a President.

A candidate's set speech, or "boilerplate," though repetitious and even banal, may provide the most useful substantive basis on which a voter can make his decision. For here, in the potential President's own words, is what he thinks the campaign is all about, the issues that he thinks are most important, the failures of the opposition that he thinks are most serious. Its full text rarely gets printed by even the leading newspapers, and it never is heard on the network news, except possibly for a brief snippet to illustrate some theme. This is because part of the definition of "news" is "new." No reporter could long survive his editor's wrath after filing a story that began, "The candidate today in Toledo said exactly the same thing he said in Seattle yesterday and in Atlanta the day before." Yet this may quite accurately reflect the event. As the campaign progresses, the reporters are caught up in a system that forces them to report more and more marginal news (size of crowds, hecklers, staff squabbles); the candidates respond—often at the urging of special interest groups— by issuing more and more statements on marginal issues. A volume published by Nixon's campaign committee in 1968

24. Arthur M. Schlesinger, Jr., *A Thousand Days* (Fawcett, 1967), p. 893. Also see Henry Fairlie, *The Kennedy Promise* (Doubleday, 1973), p. 65.

listed his views on 227 subjects divided into 43 categories. The result is a sort of Gresham's Law: the peripheral tends to push out what is central, and nothing gets very much attention, although a great deal of information is disseminated. Americans might not have been so surprised at President Nixon's overtures to Peking if his campaign speech of October 19, 1968—"We must . . . anticipate eventual conversations with the leaders of Communist China"—had not been overwhelmed in the "information clog."[25] Newspapers and TV networks should consider rotating their reporters more often; at the point that they have memorized a candidate's set speech, they are ready for another assignment. There is a certain irony in this belief that we would know more if we were not told about so many things: if a candidate was limited to, say, a half-dozen topics, by Election Day we might have a better idea of his positions on those issues he thought most important; the further irony is that to some degree it is the press representatives—asking questions on our behalf—who broaden the contents of a campaign beyond the maximum limits within which information is useful for making a rational choice. But in the likely absence of any self-censorship, it is still more ironic that our best interests are then served by an excessively long (and thus boring) campaign during which so much is said and reported that each citizen eventually should absorb that which is most helpful in the act of casting a ballot for a presidential candidate.

Although in some respects policy formulation in campaigns is handled better than we have the right to expect, given the nature of the system, and in some respects it is handled worse than we feel we deserve, given the seriousness of the decision we are asked to make, on one level the candidates' pledges are almost always honored, and the campaign is highly pre-

25. Quoted in James Keogh, *President Nixon and the Press* (Funk and Wagnalls, 1972), p. 13.

dictive. This is the symbolic level.[26] Some part of every campaign is conducted in symbols or code words, shorthand for social attitudes which cannot be easily translated into programmatic terms: DON'T LET THEM TAKE IT AWAY (Democrats, 1952); CLEAN UP THE MESS IN WASHINGTON (Republicans, 1952); A CHOICE NOT AN ECHO (Goldwater, 1964); LAW AND ORDER (Nixon, 1968); SEND THEM A MESSAGE (Wallace, 1972). Symbolic promises are easier to keep. The very act of election may be the fulfillment: "Send them a message" by electing me, says a candidate, and having elected him you have sent the message. But a President in distributing symbolic rewards is least serving as "President of all the people"; for symbolic rewards, like patronage jobs, go to the faithful or to those whom a President would like to have become faithful.

The relevance of the Tweedledee-Tweedledum argument—that there is no real difference between candidates on issues—probably depends on where one positions oneself along the ideological spectrum; most Americans are bunched in the center, although it is a floating center and sometimes hard to locate. For those near the center, the campaign—on both programmatic and symbolic levels—functions to provide even modestly attentive voters with enough information on policy to find legitimate reasons to choose which of two candidates they would prefer to have in the White House for four years. It does not furnish an elevated level of discourse; it does not provide a carefully delineated topographical map of future public policy; and it may misdirect the voters if they are led to expect more than a politician can reasonably deliver in a

26. See Moynihan, *The Politics of a Guaranteed Income*, p. 158. Donald Stokes also makes a distinction between what he calls "valence issues" ("those that merely involve the linking of the parties with some condition that is positively or negatively valued by the electorate") and "position issues." See his "Spatial Models of Party Competition," in Angus Campbell (ed.), *Elections and the Political Order* (Wiley, 1966), pp. 170–71.

system of balanced powers and at times of changeable circumstances.

The Campaign as National Self-Examination

During the presidential election year, "The nation at once celebrates and mourns itself."[27] The celebration takes the form of a reaffirmation of our national worth. "Americans have long had a novel and overwhelming need to be reassured that they are a moral and good people," Michael Novak has written. "American soldiers give chewing gum to little children. We need to think of ourselves as good, in a manner distinctly American."[28]

The presidential campaign is part of the ritual for reasserting this sense of American goodness. Politicians tell us "what is right with America." For the challenger the danger is in crossing the line between attack on policy and attack on country. This was the problem that confronted George McGovern in 1972. Public opinion polls revealed that a majority of Americans believed that our involvement in Vietnam was a mistake, while, at the same time, they saw themselves as patriotic and proud of the fact that the country "had never lost a war." In the end McGovern was unable to convince a substantial part of the electorate that his antiwar stance was patriotic.

Yet if Americans celebrate themselves in what many view as a national orgy of smugness, they also mourn themselves in what often approaches masochism. Possibly this is a form of catharsis by which campaigns serve the public good in providing the opportunity every fourth year to talk about all the awful things that have befallen the society, by getting the animosities out in the open, and by purging the body politic of some of its bile. This theory of restoration by rhetoric

27. Garry Wills, Nixon Agonistes (Signet Books, 1971), p. 46.
28. Michael Novak, The Rise of the Unmeltable Ethnics (Macmillan, 1972), p. 92.

probably applies to a very small number. For the rest of us, after listening to predictions of the apocalypse, someone gets elected and we survive—perhaps because politicians are not as bad as other politicians tell us they are, perhaps because politics is not as important as politicians would have us believe, perhaps because we were not listening very attentively, perhaps because of a healthy skepticism of what politicians tell us. There is evidence to suggest that we do discount what we are told in campaigns. A Harris Poll after Nixon's landslide victory in 1972, for example, showed that a majority of those interviewed did not believe that, despite his campaign promises, the President would either "keep the federal spending in line" or be able "to avoid increasing federal taxes."[29]

There is a dark side to self-examination. Campaigns explicate the fears of Americans—whether it be the fear of communism or the fear of walking the streets at night. Equally the campaigns put the candidates on notice as to what the electorate most fear about them—whether it be Kennedy's Catholicism or Eisenhower's military background. Our fears may be less uplifting than our hopes, but an understanding of them is not necessarily less important to the functioning of government.

The Campaign as Entertainment

The presidential campaign has a long history as entertainment: the torchlight parades with the marchers wearing oilskin capes to protect themselves from the dripping of the kerosene; the giant outdoor rallies measured in acres, ten thousand men to the acre; the dispensing of "E.C. Booz Old Cabin" and other liquid stimulants. Whether on the frontier or in the city, the campaign was different from everyday life. It was colorful and tuneful. A newspaper editor recalled the 1840 Whig campaign as "a ceaseless torrent of music, still

29. Washington Post, Dec. 28, 1972.

beginning, never ending."[30] The entertainment was functional; that is, it interested people in public affairs. It provided a pleasant diversion. And it was free.

Adam Yarmolinsky argues, "It did not detract from the intellectual content of political discourse in the 19th century that it was also designed to provide entertainment." Then he adds, "But it wasn't competing with the Johnny Carson Show."[31] Television now gives us more free entertainment than we can absorb. Moreover, entertainment in a campaign is no longer functional. In the TV competition for attention the politician is inherently disadvantaged. He has learned that he can preempt popular programs only at his own peril. He can deliver his message through spot commercials—they are unobtrusive—but they hardly raise the level of discussion, and they remind us that he has chosen a technique that is used to sell detergents and other products. Perhaps, too, politics as entertainment is less appropriate in a great nation than in an emergent nation and less fitting for a twentieth-century world leader than for a nineteenth-century parochial one.

Yet the information media increasingly have chosen to treat the political process as entertainment. Magazines and TV networks now assign celebrities to cover the conventions and the campaigns.[32] We learn from the first page of Mailer's account of the 1972 Democratic convention that it was "dismaying in its absence of theatre" and had "not enough

30. Quoted in Freeman Cleaves, Old Tippecanoe (Scribner's, 1939), p. 326.
31. Adam Yarmolinsky, "Responsible Law-Making in a Technically Specialized Society," in Geoffrey C. Hazard, Jr. (ed.), Law in a Changing America (Prentice-Hall, 1968), pp. 101–02.
32. How the candidates were doing in 1972 we learned from reading or watching Norman Mailer, Kurt Vonnegut, Jr., Germaine Greer, Joe McGinniss, Gore Vidal, John Kenneth Galbraith, and Nora Sayre. Sayre reported from the Republican convention, "I wore a dress from 1966 in order to spend a lot of time with the faithful." See "Happy Days Are Here Again," New York Times Book Review, Oct. 22, 1972.

drama."[33] To some degree the search for drama reflects the politicizing of the literati. But it is mainly the result of television's impact as the prime conveyor of mass news. In contrast to the established routine of newspaper journalism (who, what, where, when, how), the "principal need [of television reporting] is for a clear, continuous narrative line sustained throughout the story—something with a beginning, a middle, and an end that will create, maintain, and if possible increase the viewer's interest (otherwise, he might switch to another channel)."[34] It is possible, of course, that TV coverage and other reportage will restore the functional role of entertainment to the campaign. One would like to think so: most Americans have never confused solemnity with seriousness. Still the odds are overwhelming that in the long run politicians will never again be able to compete as free entertainment. Nor should we expect them to do so. Where once the political process was enhanced by being entertaining, now the attempt to entertain merely detracts from the primary purpose. Though campaigns may be a bore, we are more likely to be bored when we expect to be entertained and are not. We do not expect to be entertained by a vote in Congress, a Supreme Court decision, or an executive order. And we are not disappointed.

33. Mailer, *St. George and the Godfather*, p. 3.
34. Paul H. Weaver, "Is Television News Biased?" *Public Interest*, No. 26 (Winter 1972), p. 67.

FIVE

Communications

☆ ☆ ☆ ☆ ☆ ☆ ☆ ☆ ☆ ☆ ☆ ☆ ☆ ☆ ☆ ☆

What are the influences and effects of television and other changes in communications on the presidential selection process? When the electorate receives its information in new ways and when the candidates deliver their messages in new ways, new possibilities for distortion creep into the system . . .

REPEATEDLY since the early 1950s journalists, writers of fiction, and academics have predicted that the United States is about to experience a "neo-Orwellian revolution" that will result in "the electronic programming of the political process."[1] *The Golden Kazoo*, a novel by John G. Schneider published in 1956, tells how an advertising campaign for a presidential candidate manipulates the voters; Frank Skeffington, the protagonist of Edwin O'Connor's *The Last Hurrah*, loses his race for mayor of Boston because he cannot adjust to the political impact of television; in 1962 Edward A. Rogers, Nixon's TV consultant, wrote *Face to Face*, a novel in which a network executive technologically sabotages a candidate for President during a televised debate; Eugene Burdick's 1964 presidential campaign novel, *The 480*, recounts manipulation by computer.[2] A typical forecast, made

1. See Frederick G. Dutton, *Changing Sources of Power: American Politics in the 1970s* (McGraw-Hill, 1971), p. 196.
2. In the novels of Schneider and Burdick, the manipulation is done on behalf of a Republican presidential candidate. This may reflect the Republicans' earlier use of the new technology. There is a touch of irony,

by Holman Hamilton in 1958, states, "In the future as in the recent past it is likely that masters of merchandizing techniques will attempt to package and sell candidates as effectively as they package and sell breakfast foods and deodorizers."[3] This is the message of Vance Packard and Joe McGinniss.[4] One of the best college introductory textbooks warns, "The impact of television on American politics since 1952 should not be underestimated."[5] Judging from the literature, this has never been a problem.

John Lindsay, the most "telegenic" candidate ever to seek a presidential nomination, and one who used TV extensively in his campaign, was ignominiously defeated in all the primaries he entered in 1972; Richard Nixon, possibly our least "telegenic" candidate, carried forty-nine states in winning a second presidential term. The most infamous commercial in a presidential contest, the "Daisy Girl" spot, made for Lyndon Johnson in 1964, was shown only once, and if everyone who saw it had voted for Barry Goldwater, the election would still have gone to Johnson.[6]

The "reach" of TV, of course, is considerable. Almost every home has at least one set, and most Americans judge it their prime source of news. But as a commercial enterprise,

---

however, in the fact that Burdick's novel clearly was modeled on work done for John F. Kennedy. See Ithiel de Sola Pool, Robert P. Abelson, and Samuel L. Popkin, *Candidates, Issues, and Strategies: A Computer Simulation of the 1960 and 1964 Presidential Elections* (M.I.T. Press, 1964).

3. Holman Hamilton, *White House Images and Realities* (University of Florida Press, 1958), p. 62.

4. See Packard, *The Hidden Persuaders* (McKay, 1957), and McGinniss, *The Selling of the President 1968* (Trident, 1969).

5. Milton C. Cummings, Jr., and David Wise, *Democracy under Pressure* (Harcourt Brace Jovanovich, 1971), p. 298.

6. The commercial was run during NBC's "Monday Night at the Movies" on Sept. 7, 1964. It showed a little girl plucking daisy petals while a doomsday voice begins a countdown, followed by a mushroom cloud and the voice-over of President Johnson reminding listeners that "these are the stakes." See Theodore H. White, *The Making of the President 1964* (Atheneum, 1965), p. 322.

selling air time to candidates to sell themselves to the voters, television has never caused the nomination of a presidential candidate or the election of a presidential nominee.

The expectation that presidential candidates are going to be sold successfully like breakfast food rests on three assumptions: (1) that "media manipulators" know how to sell candidates; (2) that voters are willing to swallow a sales pitch; and (3) that candidates are willing to be sold like breakfast food. All three are dubious propositions.

The advertising profession has had "few inhibitions against the propagation of myths that inflated its own capabilities."[7] Many grandiose claims have been little more than self-advertisements by those seeking political clients. Initially presidential candidates did employ commercial advertising agencies, and the early "ads," as Stanley Kelley's analysis of the 1952 Eisenhower-Stevenson contest illustrates, were not very different from attempts to sell breakfast food.[8] Recently the advertising agencies of limited political instinct have been replaced by media consultants who specialize in politics or by ad hoc agencies put together by candidates for the sole purpose of producing their media campaigns. Since many of these "new politics" consultants do not receive commissions from the broadcasters for buying the candidates' air time, as is the practice with advertising agencies, there is less pressure on the candidates to spend their media budgets on TV. Less TV time was purchased in 1972 than in 1968. Instead, the 1972 campaigns placed heavy emphasis on direct mail (in part because new technology increased the effectiveness of direct mail; in part because the Federal Election Campaign

7. V. O. Key, Jr., *Public Opinion and American Democracy* (Knopf, 1961), p. 6.

8. Example of a 1952 commercial:
VOICE: Mr. Eisenhower, what about the high cost of living?
EISENHOWER: My wife, Mamie, worries about the same thing. I tell her it's our job to change that on November 4.
See Stanley Kelley, Jr., *Professional Public Relations and Political Power* (Johns Hopkins Press, 1956), p. 189.

Act of 1971 exempted direct mail from spending limitations).[9]

To some degree the new breed of political manager is more
restrained in claims for the selling power of TV. Perhaps this
is because research has shown that TV viewers are highly
self-selective. Most studies agree that "people pay attention
primarily to content that already interests them and that is
congenial to their point of view."[10] Political television commercials on the presidential level thus tend to be reinforcing,
rather than converting, and candidates have to use them
defensively, because their opponents use them. There is even
some evidence to suggest that candidate visibility on TV is
counterproductive: the more a candidate is seen, the less
attractive he becomes.

Moreover, each side now has its own "media manipulator,"
theoretically canceling out his opposite number. These experts do not lack theories about which techniques work and
which ones do not. But in the absence of hard facts to sub-
stantiate competing claims, media consultants tend to promote those approaches that they think were successful in the
last election. The cinéma vérité or documentary style pi-
oneered by Charles Guggenheim was considered extremely
effective during the 1960s for such candidates as Milton
Shapp, Pat Brown, and Robert Kennedy. It also spawned a

9. Another imaginative use of the media in 1972 was largely overlooked by the press. This was the purchase of radio time by Nixon to
deliver fourteen addresses. This technique met many of the criticisms of
presidential campaigning: the speeches were directed to issues; they were
long (fifteen minutes); they used a medium (radio) that places less emphasis on personality than TV; and they were economical in terms of
cost per listener.

10. Kurt Lang and Gladys Engel Lang, Politics and Television (Quadrangle, 1968), p. 16. "Certainly it is clear from the evidence which social
science has compiled thus far," write Harold Mendelsohn and Irving
Crespi, "that the injection of high doses of political information during
the frenetic periods of national campaigns does very little to alter the
deeply rooted, tightly held political attitudes (or prejudices) of most
voters." Polls, Television, and the New Politics (Chandler, 1970), p. 248.

host of imitators. Then because the public tired of repetition, initial effectiveness was based on novelty, the imitators lacked the creativity of the originator, or some other reason, the technique seemed to lose its potency and now can be expected to be followed by another wave of theories as to how TV can be used to influence voters.

Most important has been the resistance of voters to the sales pitch. At a time when illiteracy is statistically insignificant, when virtually every American of high school age now graduates from a high school, and when almost half of all Americans of college age now enter college, voters are less likely prospects to be indoctrinated, manipulated, or subliminally influenced in their choice of Presidents. They know when they are seeing a "commercial," and they adjust accordingly. Yet a demeaning view of a gullible electorate persists: as stated in a recent academic study, "Though it may not yet be possible to fool all of the people all of the time, the distressing thought that such a possibility might be enhanced by recent developments in televised political advertising accounts for some of the growing apprehension concerning those developments." The evidence given of "those developments" was a news magazine article on the TV commercials of three senatorial candidates—two of whom lost, while the winner was generally recognized as being superior to his opponent.[11] Studies that stress the ignorance of the

11. See Robert L. Peabody and others, *To Enact a Law: Congress and Campaign Financing* (Praeger, 1972), pp. 12–13 (italics added). The authors are correct, of course, if they mean that allowing a candidate to present his message on film provides special opportunities to distort, but this hardly justifies a belief that politicians may someday "fool all of the people all of the time."

A survey of ticket-splitting voters during the 1970 gubernatorial election in Michigan ranked TV ads as twenty-fourth among the factors that they said influenced them. See Walter DeVries and Lance Tarrance, Jr., *The Ticket-Splitter* (Eerdmans, 1972), p. 78. "The major fallacy in that [survey]," says political media consultant Robert Goodman, "is that no red-blooded American will ever confess to an interviewer that what he saw on a television spot persuaded him." Quoted in Lewis W. Wolfson, "The Media Masters," *Washington Post*, Feb. 20, 1972 (*Potomac* supplement, p. 15).

electorate on specific issues should not be interpreted as meaning that voters do not rationally sort out the issues that are of greatest concern to them or the qualities in a candidate that they sense would be most supportive. In 1960, for example, Nixon received 58 percent of the Negro vote in Atlanta; in 1964 Goldwater received less than 1 percent of that vote. Many of these voters may not have known the substance of the Civil Rights Act of 1964, many may not have known that Goldwater voted against it. But their massive vote-shift suggests that they had a firm notion of which candidate was most sympathetic to their interests. In the words of V. O. Key, "[V]oters are not fools."[12]

Also overlooked sometimes is the resistance of candidates to being merchandised and sold. Rockefeller during the crucial 1964 California primary and Goldwater in that fall's campaign canceled TV presentations of films that their staffs had produced, because they found them to be in questionable taste and not in the public interest.[13]

Candidates, of course, do spend immense sums on TV and do make adjustments in their presentations and schedules. (They will now plan a "visual event" in the morning, for example, so as to increase their chances of being seen on the evening news.) But the typical barnstorming campaign—despite increased risks of assassination—suggests that improved transportation technology affects the candidates' uses of their own time more than does improved communications tech-

12. V. O. Key, Jr., *The Responsible Electorate* (Harvard University Press, 1966), p. 7.
13. For an account of the Goldwater film, see Karl Hess, *A Cause That Will Triumph* (Doubleday, 1967), p. 140, and Stephen Shadegg, *What Happened to Goldwater?* (Holt, Rinehart and Winston, 1965), pp. 254–55; for an account of the Rockefeller film, see Gene Wyckoff, *The Image Candidates* (Macmillan, 1968), pp. 179–87. Although Joe McGinniss in *The Selling of the President 1968* stressed the guile of advertising men in trying to "package" Nixon, an underlying theme is that "Nixon had never liked the idea of advertising men giving him an image" (pp. 78–79). The same point is made by John Osborne, "Nixon through the Tube," in *The First Two Years of the Nixon Watch* (Liveright, 1971), pp. 105–08 (first year).

nology. An explanation would have to take into account the politician's strong sense of tradition. There are ancient and deeply ingrained tribal rituals in political campaigning. All candidates for President to date, having to be at least thirty-five years of age, grew up in a nontelevision society. It is possible that future generations of candidates will be more attuned to TV's potential. Yet William Jennings Bryan, the inventor of the whistlestop campaign, has influenced politicians who could never have seen him and are undoubtedly unaware of his effect on how they run for office; they are part of a continuum of behavior, and any changes come gradually.

The sheer chaos of the presidential selection process also acts as a powerful check against "media manipulation." Under the U.S. system, the candidates propose themselves, build their own organizations to secure their nominations, raise their own funds, are not anointed by their parties until late in the season, and, during the period of maximum voter interest, are competing for attention with thousands of claimants for lesser elective positions. The permanent party organizations are weak and cannot support a candidate before the conventions (unless he is an incumbent). There is a very high turnover of players every four years—candidates, staff, experts. Even experienced politicians generally are novices at running for President. An advertising campaign for a commercial product is based on long-range planning, allocation of resources, continuity, and usually brand-name identification. These factors hardly exist in presidential election politics. There would be greater risk of manipulation under a parliamentary system with a strong permanent party organization, the capability for a continuous "selling" campaign, and voter selection between the equivalent of brand names, whether Conservative and Liberal or Democratic and Republican.

The principal effect that TV as a commercial medium might have in presidential selection politics has not been tested. Recent experience—such as the campaigns of Howard

Metzenbaum (Senate, Ohio, 1970) or Milton Shapp (Governor, Pennsylvania, 1966)—is that relatively unknown, heavily financed candidates can win statewide primaries largely through skillful use of television. What TV can do well is build name-recognition. Guggenheim, who worked in several underdog campaigns, says, "There's a phenomenon in American politics [in state primaries] which television has emphasized: men who have no record are often more appealing than men who have a record. . . . TV dramatizes this political virginity. Before there was television, an unknown couldn't run at all because he couldn't get the exposure. With television, he can become known in a very short time."[14] The technology exists to make it easier for a non-politician to accumulate respectable showings in early presidential primaries. Such a person probably would have to be otherwise credible, perhaps through distinction in nonelective public service. Thus TV has the latent capacity to increase the number of people seeking presidential nominations.

Even if two decades of experience with TV in presidential elections has proved to be less hazardous to the health of the body politic than early forecasts suggested, television's potential for manipulation is the sort of concern that deserves constant attention. Paul A. Porter, a former chairman of the Federal Communications Commission, has proposed a five-point "code of ethics" for paid political advertising on television:

1. Broadcasters should accept no paid political messages of less than five minutes.

2. Broadcasters should reject all political advertising which contains film clips, pictures, or tape recordings of the opposing candidate, unless such opposition candidate is given an opportunity in advance to view the material and prepare an appropriate reply to be broadcast simultaneously.

3. Dramatizations of political issues should be prohibited.

4. Disparaging attacks upon a political candidate should not

14. Wolfson, "The Media Masters," p. 14.

be permitted except when personally made by an opposing candidate.

5. No new political material should be accepted by any broadcaster during the last 48 hours of the campaign.[15]

Broadcasters correctly have resisted efforts to assign them the role of political censor. Though the aims of Porter's code are laudable—a more rational discussion of issues, free of gimmicks and mudslinging—let us see how the rules would apply to a well-known commercial produced in 1972 by "Democrats for Nixon."

The scene opens with the camera on a formation of toy soldiers. "The McGovern defense plan," says the narrator. "He would cut the Marines by one-third. The Air Force by one-third. He'd cut Navy personnel by one-fourth. He would cut interceptor planes by one-half. The Navy fleet by one-half . . ." A hand comes across the screen and sweeps away the toys. "President Nixon doesn't believe we should play games with our national security," concludes the narrator.[16]

This commercial violates three of Porter's five rules. It is "disparaging," and a "dramatization," and presented in "less than five minutes." Yet how unfair is it? The size of the defense force is a legitimate issue; the differences between the candidates were notable; McGovern, although hardly playing "games," did propose precise budget cuts, which could be translated into terms of reductions in men and equipment. This Nixon commercial is what is known as a "negative" spot. Some commentators have proposed outlawing such presentations; but their objections imply that the only information voters should have to make rational decisions is "positive"—clearly not the case. Whether a candidate can present a useful message in a minute or less is not the open-and-shut case that opponents of spot commercials have made of it. Spot

15. Paul A. Porter, "Did You Know Ronald Reagan Shot Lincoln?" *Washington Post*, Jan. 23, 1972.

16. See Thomas E. Patterson and Robert D. McClure, *Political Advertising: Voter Reaction to Televised Political Commercials* (Princeton: Citizens' Research Foundation, 1974), p. 15.

commercials have been attacked as oversimplifications and distortions.[17] Distortion, however, is not inherent in the technique; there can be thirty-minute distortions. All that a spot is is short—as are most items on network news programs. A candidate can *state* an important position in a very few seconds ("I favor/oppose X"); what he cannot do is explain it thoroughly. A commercial of any length, unlike a news broadcast, is the sponsor's attempt to tell his side of the story. Like all elements of the campaign that the candidate controls—speeches, billboards, bumper stickers, flyers, direct mail, as well as radio-television-newspaper advertising—it is part of a simplification process. As such, it is nonintellectual (not necessarily anti-intellectual). When the candidate seeks to simplify he is engaged in a form of decision-making, a selecting out of certain data. He does this not necessarily because he is incapable of higher thoughts but because he seeks to reach a mass audience through mass tools. With the exception of Republican "dirty tricks" in 1972, which did not involve media manipulation, the more prominent the office sought, the less likely is the mud to be slung.[18] The style of the canvass does not profoundly affect the style of the presidency. Candidates may act as clowns; Presidents do not.

TV does provide the technology to alter the relationship between Presidents and press. "Richard Nixon believed—and more than once advised his associates—that the best way to communicate with the people was to appear on live television and speak directly to them," reports a former White House aide, James Keogh.[19] This is what he did frequently as President. Since the press sees its traditional role as conduit between President and public, Nixon's approach was a direct

17. See, for example, Alan L. Otten, "Out, Damned Spot," *Wall Street Journal*, March 9, 1972.

18. For "dirty tricks" in nineteenth-century presidential campaigns, see Eugene H. Roseboom, *A History of Presidential Elections* (Macmillan, 1957), pp. 90–91, 132–33, 270, 282–83.

19. James Keogh, *President Nixon and the Press* (Funk and Wagnalls, 1972), p. 39.

challenge to news writers. Even if Nixon had not been put on the defensive by the Watergate scandal, he would not have entirely won this battle. No President can go to the people too often—for he would bore them to death—and every President knows this.[20] Nor is the press going to go away; and so a President will try to use it for his own purposes, as every President has attempted to do in the past. Yet once a President has shown how easy it is to take his case directly to the people, all future Presidents will do it increasingly and will, in fact, find new techniques. Even though executive incumbency can be a two-edged sword, this "Nixon doctrine" could give future Presidents a decided advantage when seeking reelection.[21]

News-makers have always accused news-gatherers of excessive bias. What differentiates the current debate over TV news is that a form of communications is being accused of excessive power. "No medium has a more profound influence over public opinion," says former Vice President Agnew. "Where the New York Times reaches 800,000 people, NBC reaches twenty times that number with its evening news."[22] Power is here measured in numbers of viewers. Whether three networks should have this power to determine what is news for an estimated 43 million Americans each night is no frivolous question. Would a democracy be better served by a greater variety of news? Is it economically feasible to design a system that would provide such diversity? Agnew did not offer answers: he merely challenged the system to rid itself

20. According to Franklin Roosevelt, "People tire of seeing the same name day after day in the important headlines of the papers, and the same voice night after night over the radio. . . . Individual psychology cannot, because of human weakness, be attuned for long periods of time to a constant repetition of the highest note in the scale." Quoted in Arthur M. Schlesinger, Jr., The Politics of Upheaval (Sentry Books, 1966), pp. 9–10.

21. See Stephen Hess and Thomas E. Cronin, "The Incumbent as Candidate," Washington Post, Aug. 20, 1972.

22. Speech of Vice President Spiro Agnew, Des Moines, Iowa, Nov. 13, 1969.

of what he felt were biases, leaving the question of power unaddressed. TV makes it more and more difficult for Americans to escape from politics. Each citizen sees a great deal more of his political leaders than ever before. But, as Agnew claims, does this make TV a profound influence over public opinion? Documenting TV's influence in presidential campaigns, other than by counting numbers of viewers, is extremely difficult. Reuven Frank, a former president of NBC News, has said that "there are events which exist in the American mind and recollection primarily because they were reported on regular television news programs."[23] Television may have long-term effects; it seems logical to expect that constant exposure to certain persons or issues will eventually have public consequences, and it is only that we have not learned to measure them. But as for the presidential selection process, there is no evidence that TV news has caused the nomination or election of a single candidate.[24]

It has been contended that the TV debates of 1960 elected Kennedy. Samuel Lubell's analysis finds that "the debates did not bring any basic change in the voting pattern of the nation."[25] Yet in an election in which the popular vote margin was 113,000 out of 68.8 million votes cast, any single factor—including the debates—could have made the difference. It is estimated that 80 percent of the adult population heard at least one of the debates. Although such tremendous interest

23. Quoted in Edward Jay Epstein, "Onward and Upward with the Arts: The Selection of Reality," New Yorker, Vol. 49 (March 3, 1973), p. 42.

24. A study of the influence of TV news in the 1972 campaign concludes, "Television news could not have contributed to voter change on most campaign issues simply because it failed to adequately cover most campaign issues." Robert D. McClure and Thomas E. Patterson, "Television News and Voter Behavior in the 1972 Presidential Election" (paper delivered at the 1973 annual meeting of the American Political Science Association).

25. Samuel Lubell, "Personalities vs. Issues," in Sidney Kraus (ed.), The Great Debates (Peter Smith, 1968), p. 160. Contra, see Pierre Salinger, With Kennedy (Doubleday, 1966), p. 47.

should have translated into increased voter turnout, the percentage of Americans casting a ballot in 1960 was only 1 point higher than in 1964, when there were no debates. Moreover, debates of the 1960 variety raise troubling questions: do they overemphasize personality, the candidate as actor? McLuhan viewed the contents of the 1960 debates as irrelevant but judged them decisive in terms of image, "the shy young sheriff" versus "the railway lawyer."[26] Even if TV debates between presidential candidates are in the public interest, the odds are against their taking place unless they are required by law. This is because all or most of five conditions must be met before the candidates can be expected to agree to debate: the candidates must be on relatively even terms; they must both feel they could gain by debating; both candidates must believe themselves good debaters; neither candidate must be the incumbent; and there must be only two major candidates in the race. Rarely will circumstances line up in this way.

Why does a communications system that reaches so many affect so few? The following are four interrelated suggestions:

Network television is a commercial venture. Entertainment will always be the dominant fare. This is where the networks make their money, and this will limit the amount of news offered. The evening news broadcasts may break even or be marginally profitable; documentaries and other extended public affairs presentations always will be shown at a substantial loss. Not only are documentaries viewed by a small segment of the potential audience, but, probably more important from the viewpoint of a network's balance sheet, they diminish audiences in adjacent time periods. Reviewing media coverage of the 1972 presidential race, Ben Bagdikian writes, "[T]he most significant change in network behavior in this campaign was the almost complete disappearance of prime-time political specials on issues between Labor Day and Elec-

26. Marshall McLuhan, *Understanding Media* (McGraw-Hill, 1964), p. 330.

tion Day."[27] Besides limiting the *amount* of news presented, the commercial nature of the networks may also have an effect on the *substance* of the news presented. The evening news programs are aired at suppertime, and the often bland character of the views presented suggests that the networks are perhaps concerned with producing news-to-eat-by.[28]

Television is a government-regulated industry. Because of FCC regulations and the fear of sanctions, public affairs broadcasting by the networks is less opinionated than that which is offered by other news media. One TV critic has posited that a television documentary on whether the world is flat or round would conclude: "The world is not flat. . . . We don't say it is round either. . . . We have just presented both sides of the controversial issue. You determine just what the world is."[29] In political campaigns, the FCC's "equal time" provision—requiring stations to give all candidates for the same office, including those of minor parties, the same amount of free time—and its "fairness doctrine"—stating that the expression of one opinion must be balanced by a station with the expression of contrasting opinions—can provide the excuse for stations to present no opinion at all.

Television is the most "mass" of all media. The appeal that the networks think they must make is to so broad an audience that this affects the sophistication of analysis, choice of subject matter, tolerance of deviant opinion (affiliated stations have the right to reject network programming), and the degree to which they are willing to take sides on any issue. The format of the networks' news programs may contribute to their mass appeal but not to an enlightened citizenry. The average story is seen for 100 seconds, an inadequate amount of time to explain an issue of complexity.

27. Ben H. Bagdikian, "The Fruits of Agnewism," *Columbia Journalism Review* (January–February 1973), p. 19.
28. See Robert MacNeil, "The News on TV and How It Is Unmade," *Harper's* (October 1968).
29. Marvin Kitman, *The Marvin Kitman TV Show* (Outerbridge and Lazard, 1972), p. 14.

Television is a captive of its own technology. It is a visual medium. TV tells stories essentially through pictures. A fire or a riot can be easily visualized; it is more difficult to present —simply and quickly—a moving picture of the "gold drain" or "impoundment." There is a subtle preference for news that focuses on action rather than ideas, and this limits the influence that TV can have in shaping political debate. Moreover, TV is a constantly moving series of pictures; image follows image as on a continuous conveyor belt. The medium cannot program thinking time or learning time. Even if a profound thought is presented, the picture cannot be stopped to give the listener an opportunity to absorb its significance. The technology of TV—particularly film editing—has created a new concept of time. "Television time," like a Mack Sennett chase, is a speeded-up version of reality, a concentration of data that does away with the repetition and pause of human communications. It is the viewers' expectations of things happening in television time that make the interview program so painfully dull. Thoughtful political discourse always will be too slow-moving to compete on commercial television time.[30]

If future Presidents continue to go "over the heads" of the news media and if the people increasingly get their headlines from the twelve-items-in-twenty-three-minutes format of the evening news on network television, what role does this leave for the daily newspapers? The better papers appear to be moving toward more in-depth interpretative reporting and away from the who-what-where-when-how journalism that has been the staple of news-gathering in the United States. Clues

30. Any discussion of the impact of TV on the political process should at least mention that the development of cable TV, with its ability to greatly expand the number of channels, has the potential to widen appreciably the variety of news available, including the possibilities of "raw news," such as the unedited speeches of presidential candidates. It might also encourage the networks to further limit their unprofitable public affairs programming. See the report of the Sloan Commission on Cable Communications, *On the Cable* (McGraw-Hill, 1971), esp. Chap. 8.

pointing in this direction were apparent in the 1972 presidential campaign coverage of such pace-setting publications as the *Washington Post* and the *New York Times*. Both papers made highly intelligent use of public opinion survey data which they commissioned; series of articles viewed the election from the vantage points of the voters, not just the politicians; the candidates' TV commercials were covered as news on a regular basis; there was greater emphasis on "team" coverage, with a group of reporters surrounding a topic from various angles; and, in the case of the *Post*, relentless investigations ultimately "broke" the Watergate case. Since the *Times* and the *Post* syndicate their stories, their impact is widely felt throughout the country.

Columnists and national political reporters have a unique role in presidential election politics that has almost nothing to do with the general public. As the nation gets larger and the selection process gets more diffused—increasing the complexity and the number of participants—some journalists have assumed a function once assigned to traditional political brokers, the "bosses." This takes a number of forms:

• At the simplest level, they act as the connective link between politicians, passing along messages that once might have been communicated in "smoke-filled rooms." When Nixon wished to cue the political community that he was considering Agnew for Vice President in 1968, he "planted" the story with David S. Broder of the *Washington Post*. Or when McGovern wished to suggest that Eagleton should get off the ticket, he gave a not-for-attribution interview to Jules Witcover of the *Los Angeles Times*. Several weeks later when Witcover was asked why he had been selected, he replied, "I guess it's because I represent a large West Coast newspaper and Eagleton was on the Coast at the time."[31]

31. Timothy Crouse, "The Boys on the Bus," *Rolling Stone* (Oct. 12, 1972), pp. 54, 56, 58. See also Richard Dougherty, *Goodbye, Mr. Christian: A Personal Account of McGovern's Rise and Fall* (Doubleday, 1973), pp. 197–98.

• As Broder points out in a brilliant essay on political reporters, they now act as "talent scouts," a prerogative that
belonged almost exclusively to politicians in the nineteenth
century.[32] In addition to informing the public on the activities of the presidential contenders, they tell the politicians
who *should be* considered for the presidency. (The candidacy
of Wendell Willkie, cited earlier, illustrates how the press
contributes to expanding the talent pool.)

• Political journalists play a large part in devising the rules
by which the contenders for a nomination are rated, both by
the public and by politicians. An example of the reporter as
"rules maker" is the designation of the "decisive primary."
Not all primaries are equally important, of course, but the
weighting is not necessarily in terms of the number of delegates at stake. At some point a primary becomes decisive in
the press corps' opinion, although it is not the same one every
fourth year. Harold Stassen in 1948 won primary victories
over Dewey in Wisconsin, Nebraska, and Pennsylvania, only
to lose the so-called decisive primary in Oregon. In 1964
Goldwater lost primaries in New Hampshire and Oregon but
won the decisive primary in California. For Stevenson in 1956
the decisive primary was Florida; for John Kennedy in 1960
it was West Virginia. In the same manner, good showings in
New Hampshire by McCarthy (1968) and McGovern (1972)
became "triumphs," whereas the winners of those primaries
(Johnson and Muskie, respectively) were awarded "setbacks"
by the press. Television correspondents now contribute to this
process. A study of network news treatment of the contenders
for the 1972 Democratic nomination shows that much of the
coverage was in terms of "front-runner" (Muskie), "under-

32. See David S. Broder, "Political Reporters in Presidential Politics,"
in Charles Peters and Timothy J. Adams (eds.), *Inside the System*
(Praeger, 1970), esp. pp. 11–15. Other roles that Broder feels the press
assumes are "summarizer of the candidate's positions," "race caller or
handicapper," "public defender," and, sometimes, "unpaid assistant campaign manager."

dog" (McGovern), "regional" candidate (Wallace), and other thematic orderings of how well a candidate was doing and how likely he was to be selected.[33] Politicians try to influence the reporters' interpretations, but generally they accept the press as the final arbiter. This power of the press grows in direct proportion to the proliferation of state primaries, which swelled to twenty-three in 1972 (a gain of seven over 1968); presumably it would be less pervasive in a national primary system.

• Finally, the columnists act as political advisers to the contenders. Their opinions can be read by anyone who buys a newspaper, yet the contents suggest that they are often writing for a more limited audience. During the struggle for the 1972 Democratic nomination, James Reston suggested that McGovern might choose "Wilbur Mills as his running mate to pacify the South"; Tom Braden proposed a "deal" for McGovern to make with George Wallace ("perhaps Secretary of the Treasury"); and Tom Wicker advised Muskie that the best way for him to get the nomination would be to drop out of the primaries.[34] Though there is nothing new about the press acting in this capacity, the popularity of Theodore White's series on The Making of the President, starting in 1960, has caused the public to become more aware

33. See James R. Ferguson and Marc F. Plattner, Report on Network News' Treatment of the 1972 Democratic Presidential Candidates (Bloomington, Ind.: Alternative Educational Foundation, 1972).

34. See James Reston, "After California," New York Times, June 7, 1972; Tom Braden, "Scenario with George Wallace," Washington Post, May 30, 1972; Tom Wicker, "What Center?" New York Times, April 27, 1972. A somewhat uncharitable view of this activity is expressed by Martin F. Nolan, chief of the Washington bureau of the Boston Globe: "Many—though by no means all—syndicated columnists now fill the frankly partisan role that minor newspapers held in the early days of the republic. They are mouthpieces for ideological factions in a party, originally dependent for their sources and prestige on chumminess with or employment under a major political figure." See "Faust at the Racetrack: Let the Reader Beware," in Frederick Dutton (ed.), Playboy's Election Guide, 1972 (Playboy Press, 1972).

of the preconvention jockeying and the press more anxious to join in the process.[35]

So columnists and political reporters have become an integral part of the presidential selection process, moving from the sidelines to the playing fields. An important columnist, whose views are read regularly in Washington and New York, is now more influential than the average governor or senator; not because he reaches masses of people, but because he is looked to by politicians as rules maker, talent scout, and adviser. Television correspondents and even anchormen, although better known to the public, play a more passive role, given the characteristics of their medium.

Despite the tremendous changes in communications technology in the twentieth century, there has been no "neo-Orwellian revolution" in the presidential selection process. The modern presidential campaign was invented in 1896 by William Jennings Bryan and Marcus Alonzo Hanna. The contribution of Bryan, the thirty-six-year-old Democratic nominee, was to personally take his cause to the people. Traveling in a private railroad car, misnamed *The Idler*, he averaged 80,000 spoken words daily, and, Bryan figured, by election day he had logged 18,009 miles, delivering some 600 speeches to perhaps five million people in twenty-seven states. (His Republican opponent, William McKinley, stuck with political orthodoxy, conducting a "front porch" campaign from his home in Canton, Ohio.) The contribution of Hanna, a Cleveland industrialist turned Republican National Chairman, was of a different dimension: he systematized and

35. A member of the national political press corps, James M. Perry, has severely criticized his colleagues for adopting a Theodore White approach to covering the campaigns. "We have become nit-pickers, peeking into dustry corners, looking for the squabbles, celebrating the trivia, and leaping to those sweeping, cosmic, melodramatic conclusions and generalities that mark the Teddy White view of American politics." See *Us & Them: How the Press Covered the 1972 Election* (Clarkson N. Potter, 1973), pp. 9–10.

brought order to the technical management of presidential campaigns. Mark Hanna ended the chaos of fund raising by levying regular assessments on the financial community; he streamlined the speakers' bureau, which recruited, trained, and scheduled 1,400 party orators; he devised a system of "surrogate" candidates who took to the hustings in place of McKinley; he assigned a speaker to trail Bryan as a sort of Republican "truth squad." Hanna's Bureau of Publications distributed 120 million pieces of literature in thirteen languages, including Hebrew; press releases and mats were sent to county newspapers with a combined circulation of five million. Hanna divided the electorate into voting blocs, assigning a staff and a budget to each, so that within the Republican National Committee there were operations specifically directed at women (who had been given the vote in Colorado, Wyoming, and Utah), Negroes, Germans, traveling salesmen, even bicyclists. Through competitive bidding, central purchasing, and strict audits, Hanna trimmed the waste factor by half. Key states were polled repeatedly to determine changes in public opinion, and what the pollsters missed was undoubtedly picked up by Hanna's spies at Democratic headquarters.

What has happened since 1896 has been the adaptation of technology in ways that have retained the traditional features of the canvass. There have been no basic changes in politics comparable, for example, to the changes in art brought about by the cubists. In 1972 Hanna would have been at ease running Nixon's campaign as would have been Bryan in McGovern's role.

SIX Money

☆ ☆ ☆ ☆ ☆ ☆ ☆ ☆ ☆ ☆ ☆ ☆ ☆ ☆ ☆ ☆

> Can a method of raising and regulating money
> in politics be devised that will encourage good
> people to run for office, eliminate corruption,
> and create a healthier political climate? The
> national reaction to Watergate has created a
> unique opportunity for enacting corrective
> legislation . . .

THE REVELATIONS about fund-raising abuses
by Nixon supporters followed the passage of the most com-
prehensive set of campaign regulations ever enacted by Congress, the Federal Election Campaign Act of 1971, which
provided for spending limitations and disclosure of campaign
contributions.[1] Changes made in the 1971 Revenue Act were
also in force at the time, permitting tax credits or tax deduc-
tions for political contributions at all levels.[2] These two pieces
of legislation came relatively close to fulfilling the recom-

1. Public Law 92-225, enacted February 7, 1972 (86 Stat. 3), among
many provisions, limits the amounts candidates may spend on communications media, limits a candidate's broadcast advertising to 60 percent of
his media expenditure, requires a broadcaster to charge candidates the
lowest unit rate charged other advertisers, places ceilings on contributions
of a candidate or his family to his campaign, requires reporting of all
contributions and expenditures over $100, and requires the registering of
all political committees with receipts over $1,000.
2. Public Law 92-178, enacted December 10, 1971 (85 Stat. 497),
allows political contributors to claim a federal tax credit for 50 percent
of their contributions up to a maximum of $12.50 on a single return and
$25 on a joint return; or to claim a deduction for the full amount of con-
tributions up to $50 (single return) and $100 (joint return).

76

mendations of President Kennedy's Commission on Campaign Costs (1962) and other moderate reformers. Indeed the Campaign Act so nearly met the reformist agenda that only three items were compromised and would remain to be enacted if Congress chose to expand this approach.[3]

True, the Campaign Act did not go into effect until April 7, 1972, and some of the Nixon committee operations were made in an effort to collect and spend money before the new measure became operative, but this is not a situation that can be repeated now that the act is in effect. Thus the scandals of 1972 can be cited to "prove" that the reforms work in that violators were exposed and prosecuted. Or the very same events can be interpreted as showing that the reforms do not work in that they failed to deter violators. Or, from another point of view, it can be argued that the whole approach—regulated private campaign financing—is bankrupt and must be replaced by a new system of public subsidy.

Clearly Americans are deeply troubled by the high cost of running for office and by the potential influence of large contributors.

The total spent on elective and party politics for all purposes at all levels in the past six presidential election years has been estimated at $140 million (1952), $155 million (1956), $175 million (1960), $200 million (1964), $300 million (1968), and $400 million (1972), with probably $100

3. The three items deleted from the 1971 Campaign Act which deserve reconsideration are: (1) repeal of Section 315 of the Federal Communications Act, the equal-time provision, which would facilitate candidate debates on TV; (2) creation of an independent electoral commission with prosecutory authority to administer the law; and (3) placing expenditure limits on additional types of campaign activities (for example, the act does not affect amounts that can be used for mass mailings). Experience with the new law during the 1972 campaign also suggests the need for administrative "fine tuning," such as requiring a contributor to list his social security number so that multiple gifts can be more easily aggregated. See Jeffrey M. Berry and Jerry Goldman, "Congress and Public Policy: A Study of the Federal Election Campaign Act of 1971," *Harvard Journal of Legislation*, Vol. 10 (January 1973).

million spent on the presidential level. In 1976, if both parties have contested nominations, the costs are likely to go even higher than straight-line projections would indicate. Regardless of the purposes for which these sums are being expended, many people are offended by their magnitude.

The causes for the rising cost of politics have been identified by David W. Adamany and others as an expanding population and electorate; more offices being filled by elections (over 500,000); disintegration of the political parties (where organizations are effective, campaigns cost less); the rise of independent voting and ticket splitting; inflation (the costs of services that candidates buy have risen faster than the costs of raw materials and finished goods); use of advanced technology (television, computerized mail, public opinion surveys), which has tended to result in add-on expenses instead of replacements for established campaign activities. Heightened competition within and between parties is a factor (more money is spent if elections or nominations are hotly contested), as is intensity over issues such as civil rights and Vietnam. Reapportionment has played a part, as well as the increased use of primaries (rather than conventions) as a means of selecting candidates. Furthermore, affluence and improved fund-raising techniques have brought in more money,[4] and the availability of money has itself created more spending.

Some of these causes are unrelated to politics (inflation, population increase); some are supportive of the democratic process (competition, primaries); some expenses could be reduced by changes that must be considered on bases other than cost (fewer elective offices, longer terms). Whether campaign costs are "too high" must depend on what Americans think elections are worth. Campaign costs as a percent of overall government costs amount to about one-tenth of 1 percent. Some observers have noted that Americans spend

4. See David W. Adamany, *Campaign Finance in America* (Duxbury Press, 1972), pp. 51–72.

more annually on chewing gum or that Procter and Gamble spends only slightly less on advertising.[5] "Considering that every poll shows how little Americans really know about great issues," contends Tom Wicker, "and how few know anything about even the leading politicians—considering also the dismaying record of lost bond issues and defeated propositions, the immense social investments many believe needed, the remaining numbers of uncontested Congressional districts and one-party states, and the shamefully low percentage of Americans who bother to vote even in Presidential races, it can well be argued that we need to spend more, not less, on politics and the political education it entails."[6]

There is a distinct difference between the needs and problems of financing politics on the presidential level and financing politics on other levels of government: presidential politics is *overfinanced* (the capacity exists to raise more money than is needed for all major candidates to run adequate campaigns); the rest of American politics is *underfinanced*, discouraging good candidates from seeking office and limiting their ability to inform the electorate.

The higher the office sought, the easier it is to raise money. The higher the office sought, the more news (free) attention is paid. The most recent example of a responsible contender claiming that he was denied the opportunity to seek a major party presidential nomination because of a lack of funds is the case of Senator Fred Harris of Oklahoma in 1972. Yet in a year in which the Democratic nomination ultimately went to another relatively young senator from a small state, also with liberal convictions and without personal wealth, it is difficult to conclude that it was the "system" that denied

5. See Philip S. Hughes in *Federal Election Campaign Act of 1973*, Hearings before the Subcommittee on Communications of the Senate Committee on Commerce, 93 Cong. 1 sess. (1973), p. 210; John S. Saloma III and Frederick H. Sontag, *Parties* (Knopf, 1972), p. 362.

6. Tom Wicker, Foreword to Herbert E. Alexander, *Money in Politics* (Public Affairs Press, 1972), p. vii.

Harris the nomination.[7] Moreover, besides McGovern, the Democratic field included another liberal, John Lindsay, whose campaign was well financed until he did poorly in the Florida primary. Of course the amount of money available is not infinitely expandable. If one thinks of the quest for a presidential nomination as a game of musical chairs with each chair representing a position on the ideological spectrum—an analogy made by Richard Rovere in 1952—perhaps there is only enough money for one (or possibly two) players to occupy each chair.

Although the rich or those with rich friends have a head start in nomination politics, their advantage does not mean automatic success. The list of losers is replete with some of the wealthiest family names in America. The efforts of Illinois Governor Frank Lowden (who was married to George M. Pullman's daughter) to win the 1920 Republican nomination caused Walter Lippmann to write, "Lowden has all that money can buy, and he seeks now the things that money does not buy."[8] That there are things in elective politics that are not for sale may be one reason why so many rich people seek the challenge of running for office. On the other hand, the experience of Goldwater, McCarthy, Wallace, and McGovern illustrates the growing ability of candidates to finance their campaigns with large numbers of small donations. McGovern has stated that roughly 80 percent of his funds were raised by mail solicitation with an average gift of about $30. While this approach may be less fruitful for those holding centrist views, there is sufficient evidence that there is enough "emotional money," if properly solicited, to finance the presidential ambitions of any articulate and visible candidate who represents a distinctive position on either the left or the right.

Money translates into messages that candidates send to prospective voters, and candidates must be able to deliver a

7. For an opposing point of view, see David Nichols, *Financing Elections* (New Viewpoints, 1972), pp. 125–30.
8. Walter Lippmann, *Early Writings* (Liveright, 1972), p. 177.

sufficient number of messages if free elections are not to be a mockery. Therefore candidates must have adequate funding. On the presidential level, however, funds often have been more than adequate, and money has been spent beyond the point of diminishing returns.[9] No recent presidential election has been lost because the electorate did not know what a candidate stood for or what he opposed—if the candidate wanted his position known.

Russell D. Hemenway is correct in believing that "voters have come to view massive campaign expenditures as a major public disgrace."[10] The "solution" may be sought in limiting campaign spending by law, which is the direction of the 1971 act. Testimony before the Ervin Committee of rivers of money flowing into and out of the Committee for the Re-election of the President presents the most compelling reason for limiting campaign expenditures—namely, that the over-supply of money creates a climate that encourages illegal spending or, conversely, that if the money was not collected, it could not be spent (illegally or legally). Yet spending limitations raise constitutional questions—the right of free speech—as well as questions of equity and questions of chang-ing balances in the political system. Still, assuming that no presidential candidate is allowed to get away with using money illegally and assuming that each has adequate funds, the fact that spending "too much" may be a "disgrace" to the Puritan ethic must be balanced against the consideration that spending "too little" would be a "disgrace" to demo-cratic principles.

9. See Stimson Bullitt, *To Be a Politician* (Doubleday, 1961), p. 72. As for congressional races, Paul A. Dawson and James E. Zinser have reached the conclusion: "In House elections [in 1970] broadcast expendi-tures seem to contribute little to the margin of victory." What then deter-mines the level of broadcast expenditures? They believe that "candidates seek to outspend one another." See "Broadcast Expenditures and Electoral Outcomes in the 1970 Congressional Elections," *Public Opinion Quar-terly*, Vol. 35 (Fall 1971), pp. 400–01.

10. Campaign Act of 1973 Hearings, p. 168.

The problem in presidential campaigns is not that private financing prevents good candidates from making the race or even that too much money is spent (although both contentions are made). Rather, trouble arises because candidates seek funds in large amounts from people or interests who then wish preferential treatment from the government. Circumstantial evidence is abundantly available in the cases of such 1972 Nixon contributors as Robert Vesco (whose finances were being investigated by the Securities and Exchange Commission), Dwayne Andreas (who wanted a federal bank charter), the dairy industry (desirous of higher milk support prices), the Seafarers International Union (when the Justice Department was in a position to appeal the dismissal of an indictment against them), and others. Public alienation and distrust are certainly products of the belief that government activities are for sale to the highest bidder in the form of political contributions.

The vast majority of contributions to presidential campaigns are made for benign reasons: because of what a candidate stands for or because of fears of the opposition candidate; because of pressure from peers (in which case the giver's relationship to the asker, not to the candidate, is determining); because a gift confers status on the giver; because of the expectation of symbolic rewards. Even those who give in the hope of gaining a job may be few in number—a President has only some 2,700 positions to dispense, and obviously all of these do not go to contributors.[11] But the system of

11. The most controversial presidential patronage has been ambassadorial appointments, where in recent years nearly one-third of all posts have been filled by noncareer people, often large political contributors. Ambassador Charles W. Yost, a retired Foreign Service officer, has called this practice "an outrageous anachronism" and proposes that "95 percent of ambassadorial appointments should be made from the career service." Chester Bowles, a former noncareer ambassador, has defended the quality (at least in the Kennedy administration) of political appointees. The roster of distinguished nonprofessionals has included Averell Harriman, John McCloy, Douglas Dillon, and David Bruce. Following the 1973 appointment as ambassador to Luxembourg of Dr. Ruth Farkas, contribu-

private financing—and its abuses—has left the impression that undue influence is at work, and this impression, even when unfounded, erodes public confidence in the democratic order.

It might appear that what should trouble most Americans about campaign funding—the potential influence of large contributors—could be corrected by limiting the amount that an individual could give to a candidate (possibly $250 per candidate and a maximum of $1,000 that an individual could give to all campaigns in a single year). Such a proposal is based on three assumptions. The first assumption is that no politician could be unduly influenced by a small contribution. The second is that candidates could raise adequate funds in this manner, which is possibly true at the presidential level and probably would be true at other levels if Congress enacted a "service package" giving to candidates free television and radio time (either contributed by the stations or purchased for them by the government), some form of free or reduced-rate mailing privileges, and a mid-week national holiday on election day (a subsidy of campaign workers by employers). The third assumption is that a limitation on the size of contributions could be made corruption-proof (through such means as centralized control of campaign fund collection and reporting, full disclosure, a range of stiff penalties, an independent supervisory commission with complete investigatory and prosecutory authority). Yet this has been tried. The Hatch Act of 1940 placed a ceiling of $5,000 on individual contributions to a single candidate for federal office. President Kennedy's Commission and other reformist

tor of $300,000 to Nixon's re-election campaign, the Senate Foreign Relations Committee staff drafted a preliminary set of ground rules that would automatically reject anyone who had given more than $5,000 to a political candidate unless the person has "prior diplomatic experience or special training in the affairs of the country to which he is being named." See Yost, "Ambassadorships for the Highest Bidders," *Washington Post*, Nov. 29, 1972; Bowles, "Taking Exception," *Washington Post*, Dec. 7, 1972; Spencer Rich, "Senate Unit Acts To Bar Title 'Sale,'" *Washington Post*, June 8, 1973.

groups during the 1960s recommended removing the restriction, which was finally done in the 1971 act.[12] The primary reason given was that the limitation had proved unenforceable. So easy was it to find ways to evade the law that its existence on the statute books, reformers thought, contributed to an undermining of public trust in the electoral process.

Proposals to change the way that money is raised and spent in presidential campaigns, or even in all federal elections, should recognize that these contests are only part of a total political ecology. A plan to provide government funding for national candidates could adversely affect the supply of talent that might otherwise vie for state and local offices; restrictions on contributions to national candidates might result in money being rechanneled to other levels. A patchwork approach to existing regulations can close some loopholes; moreover, all politicians will proceed with caution in the wake of Watergate, and so things will appear to improve. But limitations on spending or giving will not reinvigorate the two-party system or assure good candidates or promote rational debate or assist those elements of the elective process that are woefully underfinanced. The current concern over campaign financing presents a unique opportunity to confront the needs of the entire political system.

The arguments in favor of financing politics with public monies are that this will eliminate the influence of large contributors, restore confidence in a system that has become tainted by private money, equalize the ability of all candidates to seek office without reference to their personal wealth or capacity to raise money, and free public officials from the time-consuming chore of fund raising.

The arguments against public funding are that it eliminates one type of citizen participation, switches the burden of financing from those who can afford it and have the interest

12. See *Financing a Better Election System* (New York: Committee for Economic Development, 1968), p. 53.

to many who cannot afford it and have no interest, could result in the uncontrolled proliferation of candidates attracted by "free" money whose presence might confuse the voters and fracture the political system, would be costly and difficult to administer, and might violate free speech by limiting the amount that a candidate could spend.[13]

Debate over this list of pros and cons overlooks a hidden agenda, less theoretical and more likely to be governing. How would a switch from private to public financing affect incumbents (those who hold power, wish to retain power, and must approve any change in the system), and how would it affect the electoral prospects of the two major parties?

Incumbents believe they would be hurt by a public financing system that gives the same amount to all contestants for an office. In both Senate and House races in 1972 the incumbents raised roughly twice as much as their opponents. This led John Gardner to conclude "that obtaining sufficient political financial support in our present system does not relate to whether you are a Democrat or a Republican, but rather to whether you are an incumbent or a challenger."[14] The assumption is that incumbents win because they can raise more money. Probably more correct is the conclusion that incumbents win because of the advantages of incumbency. The principal advantage is not that incumbents' campaigns are better financed but that incumbents are better known, have been longer active in public life, have done more favors, made more speeches, and otherwise impressed themselves upon the voters before the campaign even begins. Scholars believe that "most voters are not affected by political campaigns."[15] The University of Michigan Survey Research Cen-

13. See Irving Ferman, "Congressional Regulation of Campaign Spending: An Expansion or Contraction of the First Amendment?" *American University Law Review*, Vol. 22 (Fall 1972), pp. 1–38.

14. Common Cause press release, March 7, 1973, p. 13.

15. See William H. Flanigan, *Political Behavior of the American Electorate* (Allyn and Bacon, 1968), p. 98.

ter data for the 1952 and 1956 presidential elections show that "fewer than two voters in five felt they had decided in the course of the campaign proper."[16] Berelson, Lazarsfeld, and McPhee stress the degree to which children "inherit" their parents' political preferences.[17] Obviously campaigns are not superfluous; candidates fight over a relatively small percentage of undecided voters, and this can be decisive in close elections.[18] Although incumbency is more likely to be an advantage for legislators than for executives, to the degree that public financing preserves the status quo, incumbents have more to gain than do their challengers.

Incumbency aside, Republicans may think they have the most to lose from changing present financing procedures. They have the ability to raise more money than their opponents through private means. This is not in dispute, but at least one observer argues that the Democrats would be more adversely affected by any limit on campaign spending. Vic Fingerhut wrote in 1971 that "the only significant shifts of voter preferences [in the period between the conventions and election], during the last six presidential campaigns, favored the Democrats."[19] (These shifts came in 1948, 1960, and 1968.) If the principal impact of campaigns on election outcomes is to rally the partisan, campaign monies can be more productively spent by Democrats—there are more of them to rally, and they are less likely to go to the polls without prodding.

Despite the decline in voter affiliation with either party,

16. Angus Campbell and others, *The American Voter* (Wiley, 1960), p. 78.

17. Bernard R. Berelson, Paul F. Lazarsfeld, and William N. McPhee, *Voting* (University of Chicago Press, 1954), p. 137.

18. Politicians generally agree that campaign activities can account for no more than 5 percent of the vote. See the remarks by Gary Hart and Jeb Magruder in Ernest R. May and Janet Fraser (eds.), *Campaign '72: The Managers Speak* (Harvard University Press, 1973), p. 214.

19. Vic Fingerhut, "A Limit on Campaign Spending—Who Will Benefit?" *Public Interest*, No. 25 (Fall 1971), p. 4.

nearly twice as many Americans consider themselves Democrats. This advantage is most reflected in legislative bodies; among chief executives, both governors and Presidents, party labels appear to be less determining, and a rough balance has been struck. (Each party, for example, has controlled the White House half of the time since 1944.) Periodic shifts in winning elections may have little to do with money; some political analysts theorize that voters are deliberately choosing to exercise a form of checks-and-balances by splitting their tickets. Clearly the fact that Republicans outspent Democrats at all levels has not produced a Republican country. It may, however, contribute to greater competition.

Given the Democrats' advantage in registration and given the fact that competition serves a highly useful purpose in an open political system, the potential consequences of nullifying by legislation the Republicans' financial advantage deserve careful attention—especially if the Democrats' superior ability to attract contributed services (through union and youth support) is not limited at the same time. If, in fact, it is possible that public financing—equal distribution of funds and prohibitions against raising additional monies— could further skew the balance between contending forces, then we must ask whether the certification of one party as the permanent minority would be in the national interest.

Unless the Revenue Act of 1971 is changed before the 1976 presidential election, the next Democratic and Republican nominees will have the option of choosing between public and private financing. A candidate who opts for public financing will be entitled to receive an amount equal "to 15 cents multiplied by the total number of residents within the United States who have attained the age of 18." (This formula would have given $20.4 million each to McGovern and Nixon if it had been in effect in 1972.) The money will come from voluntary tax payments of one dollar per person, which accumulate over four years in a "presidential election campaign fund." If the sum collected does not equal the candidates' entitlements, the money will be prorated, and the candidates will have the right to privately raise the fall-short amounts. The plan has some serious drawbacks—it covers only presidential general elections, for example, and by giving the money directly to candidates it works against creating a more responsible party system. Nevertheless, introducing the concept of public funding into American politics in this manner is worth a trial if it is understood that what is being attempted is only a partial remedy and not a cure-all for the ailments of the electoral system, that it cannot serve as a fair test by which to measure the efficacy of government financing, and that it may have some unsatisfactory consequences because of the incremental nature of the experiment.

Designing a method of political financing that meets the objectives of public funding advocates, avoids the faults of a subsidy system, and attempts to solve some of the longer-range needs of open and competitive politics should be based on four criteria.

1. *Total approach.* Regulation of funds in politics must exist equally at all levels of government. Only across-the-board regulation will respond to the need for a redistribution of money in the elective process and counter the potential for abuse that exists where funds are relatively scarce. There is a certain paradox, given the recent scandals of presidential fund raising, in that the spiraling costs of national politics mean that even large contributors pay for a very small percentage of the overall campaign. An equal amount of money invested in state or local elections would produce more leverage. Thus a plan that limits gifts or provides for subsidy only at the top could contribute to the free flow of pollution to the lower reaches of government. A uniform system of public subsidies probably would have to be presented in Congress as a grant-in-aid program with the federal government underwriting the major share of the costs. This approach traditionally carries with it the imposition of conditions, which in this case could include limitations on private contributions,

full disclosure, equitable distribution of funds, and even provisions to facilitate registration of voters and the efficient operation of the election machinery. The dimensions of the problem are national; the parts mysteriously interrelate. To reply other than totally would be like trying to legislate only one law of thermodynamics.

2. *Adequate funding.* A system of public subsidies should give candidates sufficient funds to present their views to the electorate. The formula for devising the size of the allotments should be more sophisticated than x cents per eligible voter, recognizing that expenses will not be equal (even in races for the same office in districts with the same population). Congressional districts in Houston and New York City, for instance, may each have populations of 700,000, but the costs of 15 minutes on TV will differ as will the costs of other goods and services that a candidate has to purchase. Moreover, "sufficient funds" need not be the amounts presently being spent. Common Cause points out that an elections reform bill approved by the Senate Commerce Committee in May 1973 would have allowed senatorial candidates in 1972 to spend $36.9 million, although they actually spent $25.7 million.[20] Government subsidies should not contribute to runaway spending.

3. *Party control.* Public subsidies should be given to the political parties, rather than directly to the candidates. Obviously this could not apply in primary contests where candidates are vying for a party's nomination. In such cases it might be possible to adopt an approach similar to Senator Hart's proposal for congressional elections (S. 1103): to be eligible for public monies, contestants in primary elections would have to post a security deposit equal to one-fifth of the subsidy; the deposit would be forfeited if the candidate failed to win 10 percent of the vote; the subsidy would have

20. Morton Mintz, "Hill Rejects Delay on Strengthening Election Fund Act," *Washington Post*, June 8, 1973.

to be repaid if the candidate failed to win 5 percent of the vote; monies used for the purposes of posting deposits or repaying subsidies could not be raised in amounts exceeding $250 per individual contribution. This device is designed to deter frivolous candidacies. Adjustments might have to be made after observing how well it works. Similar provisions would have to be made to defray the expenses of minor party and independent candidates. Public subsidies must not become the means of preventing the maverick from seeking office. Yet neither should it contribute to the further atrophy of the party system, which might be the result of a law that gives general election campaign funds directly to candidates. Political parties are still our best vehicle for promoting long-term and internally consistent policy objectives. There may come a time when the needs of society will be best promoted by loosening party reins, but now the need is otherwise.

4. *Reflect complexities.* Money is not the only variable in politics. A system that seeks to control the flow of money into the elective process without attempting to factor into a subsidy formula the other reasons that candidates get elected is inequitable and likely to produce unintended results. Any public underwriting of campaign costs should reflect the complexities of the political process. Take the incumbency variable. Part of the reason that an incumbent traditionally has an edge may involve the mystique of holding office. But the incumbent's advantage is also a product of the perquisites that come with the office. A member of Congress, for example, receives office space (both in Washington and in his district), equipment, staff help, stationery, franking privileges, and travel allowances. A committee chairman or ranking minority member of a committee has greater benefits. Though these allotments are rightly given to facilitate the performance of duties, they are not without utility in the political sense. A percentage of an incumbent's nonsalary compensation should be charged to his campaign subsidy, or a challenger should receive approximately equal services at government expense.

Public funding may well be the best way to control corruption, but the risk involved is that it may seriously weaken
the underdog and thus contribute to stagnation in the system.
The underdog needs *more* money to compete on even terms.
Especially at the presidential level, where every statement of
an incumbent is automatically news and those that he deems
important are broadcast in their entirety, the right of a challenger to have the same amount of money is only the right
to have less impact on the electorate. The situation is analo-
gous to Anatole France's quip that "the law allows rich and
poor alike the right to sleep under bridges." The underdog
needs the opportunity to be able to catch up—not a guarantee
but not legislated handcuffs either.

This suggests that a *mixed* system, combining public and
private funding, offers the most useful means of financing
politics: public funding to eliminate the need for large contributions with their potential for favors-buying and to provide funds for all candidates to at least minimally state their
case; private funding in modest sums (possibly not exceeding
$250 an individual) to give the underdog an opportunity to
catch up, to meet the constitutional requirement of free
speech, and to allow room for this form of citizen participation.

How expensive is the proposed system likely to be? According to John Gardner, "The fact of the matter is that you
could finance the entire costs of two national Presidential and
congressional elections for approximately the same costs as
we presently pay for one Trident submarine."[21] Another way
to calculate costs is over a four-year elections cycle. The
amount spent on electoral and party politics for all purposes
at all levels during the 1964–67 cycle was $371 million; the
1968–71 figure was in the neighborhood of $350 million.[22]
Considering the rising costs of politics, reflected in the esti-
mates for spending in 1972, the price tag for four years of

21. Campaign Act of 1973 Hearings, p. 64.
22. See Alexander, *Money in Politics,* pp. 24–35.

public-private financing (one presidential campaign, two congressional campaigns, and all other state and local elections and party operations) is around $750 million, of which 80 percent might come from public monies—substantially less than one Trident submarine.

Will this system prevent another Watergate, or encourage good candidates to run for local offices, or instill discipline in the political parties, or strike the proper balance between officeholders and challengers? We do not know. And there is no way to learn the answers from computations or a controlled experiment at a carefully selected site. But if the questions are important enough and worth the expenditure of a great deal of money, we must proceed. Then perhaps the experience of an election cycle or two will provide some answers.[23]

23. As of mid-August 1974, it is clear that the Congress will pass a campaign financing reform bill. On April 11 the Senate voted in favor of S. 3044; the House approved H.R. 16090 on August 8. See *Campaign Practices Reports*, Vol. 1, No. 2 (Washington, D.C.: Plus Publications), for a comparison of the two bills. Whatever the final version, and if signed by President Ford, the 1974 act will not resemble the proposal set forth in this chapter. It will not be a *total approach*: the House proposes public funding of presidential elections only; the Senate bill covers presidential and congressional elections. Both bills limit individual contributions, although not as severely as proposed here; both bills set up an elections commission, although only the Senate version gives it prosecutory powers.

SEVEN   Conclusion

☆ ☆ ☆ ☆ ☆ ☆ ☆ ☆ ☆ ☆ ☆ ☆ ☆ ☆ ☆ ☆

Did "the system" fail in 1972?

THE EVENTS of Watergate, as they related to the presidential selection process, included the wiretapping and burglary of the Democratic National Committee (organized and executed by operatives of the Committee to Re-elect the President); a series of Nixon campaign efforts to sabotage contenders for the Democratic nomination (presumably designed to increase George McGovern's chances of being nominated); and illegal contributions to and expenditures by the Nixon organization. Other events, of even greater consequence to the governance of a democratic society, became enmeshed in the scandal but are outside the scope of an inquiry into how Americans choose their Presidents.

President Nixon in his April 30, 1973, address to the nation rejected the contention that Watergate represented the bankruptcy of the political system. "It was the system that has brought the facts to light and that will bring the guilty to justice—a system that in this case has included a determined grand jury, honest prosecutors, a courageous judge, and a vigorous free press." Successful prosecution of the guilty, it should be noted, does not necessarily mean that the political system is working well. Assuming, however, that the way Presidents are chosen is much the same as it has been through history, the case for Watergate as an aberration, rather than a condition caused by something inherent in the system, is that Watergate is totally unprecedented in the American experience. "Politicians have played tricks on each

93

other since politics was invented," Stewart Alsop wrote.[1] But in 185 years of presidential elections there had never been campaign corruption on this scale.

Ultimately, I believe, Watergate will be explained primarily as a failure of individuals who should have been conscious of acting illegally and should have known the possible consequences of their actions. That these were men who held high trust and upon whom society had lavished honor might cause us to ask how representative they are of the nation that produced them. If indeed they are like us, then we must find ways to contain ourselves. But a free society pays a price for assuming its own immorality. "Should we have a law against red wigs? A law compelling search of all suitcases for $100 bills?" asks Meg Greenfield. "[T]here are certain limits to what we can expect the written laws to do for us and certain dangers in trying to write laws that will cover and control every possible aspect of human malfeasance."[2] The events of Watergate were prohibited by existing law; they were committed by people who knew the law. The prescription to prevent future Watergates is not likely to be additional laws or even stiffer penalties. Stiffer penalties will reflect the seriousness that society attaches to aberrant behavior, but there is little assurance that this would have deterred those involved in the crimes of 1972. Society prescribes a negative code of conduct—"thou shalt nots"—and enforces prohibitions through its legal system. The legal system is not designed to reward those who keep the law, nor can it in most cases prevent those who wish to from breaking the law. Still, it is incumbent upon us to examine the system in the light of Watergate and to consider ways to cleanse presidential selection politics.

Even if Watergate is viewed as a failure of men, it may be that politics can cause people to act more immorally than

1. Stewart Alsop, "War, Not Politics," Newsweek (May 14, 1973).
2. Meg Greenfield, "A Trust Was Broken," Washington Post, May 18, 1973.

they might in other pursuits. There is no reason to believe, for example, that the bright young men who appeared before the Ervin Committee in 1973 were not good husbands or good parents, or otherwise failed to conduct themselves in an exemplary manner. Jerry Bruno, a leading Democratic advance man, once wrote, "[W]hen you're part of a political campaign, the stakes are as high as they come. . . . I think sometimes it's what fighting a war or playing a pro football game is like."[3] The analogies are apt. Modern warfare is often a suspension of morality, often in the name of morality; pro football is a sport in which infractions of the rules are penalized by loss of yards, rarely by banishment, so that breaking the rules becomes a calculated risk rather than an act of depravity. Moreover, it is in the nature of the ad hoc staffing arrangements of presidential campaigns to temporarily remove the participants from their "real" worlds in which they individually abide by the codes of conduct of whatever occupations engage them. This does not mean that all citizens leave their morality at home when they enter a presidential campaign; only a very small number do. But, almost without exception, they do see the world of politics as different, less enduring. And for some this makes a difference in their conduct.

Under the existing system, as I said earlier, candidates seeking a presidential nomination propose themselves, raise their own funds, and build their own organizations. When a person wishes to run for President, he must very quickly recruit a staff from among friends and others who are in a position to drop what they are doing and devote themselves to his cause for periods of up to a year. People are often "loaned" by corporations, law firms, advertising agencies, newspapers, labor unions, and trade associations. The rich often loan themselves. The young are available and do not

3. Jerry Bruno and Jeff Greenfield, *The Advance Man* (Morrow, 1971), p. 29.

cost much. After the conventions, the winning candidates' personal staffs become the nuclei of the campaign organizations. These people, who are responsible for conducting the most important free election campaign in the world, are generally amateurs in that politics is not their profession, despite varying degrees of experience. It is worth recalling the statement of Richard Neustadt, made in a somewhat different context: "The Presidency is no place for amateurs."[4]

The process of conducting a presidential campaign raises questions about individual and group ethics in an election system that lacks a professional memory. Professionalism, by definition, includes a set of standards by which one is judged and upon which depends one's status. High standards of conduct are strengthened by, if not dependent upon, continuing relationships. Yet continuity is exactly what is absent from the organization of presidential campaigns.

Instead the American system tends to divorce the presidential candidates from the political parties they represent. Television has encouraged this. So have election laws. So have legions of campaign consultants, who now can supply candidates with the services that they once received from their party organizations. So too has the predominance of foreign affairs, a special concern of Presidents but traditionally one that has been treated with bipartisan detachment. Primarily, though, this is a product of a prevailing American attitude. We have scorned the professional politician and glorified a form of political Cincinnatus, the citizen-soldier who drops his plow to wage war for his candidate. Running as a Republican or a Democrat is no longer an unalloyed asset, and so, in many cases, the candidates have chosen to turn their backs on their parties. "I'm not going to ask anybody here to vote on November the 8th because of the party label that I happen to wear," said Richard Nixon in 1960.[5] One by-

4. Richard E. Neustadt, *Presidential Power* (Wiley, 1960), p. 180.
5. *The Speeches of Vice President Richard M. Nixon*, S. Rept. 994, 87 Cong. 1 sess. (1961), Pt. 2, pp. 81–82.

product of this attitude is that the permanent party committees at the national level are anemic creatures, little more than the caretakers that keep the files, convene the conventions, and dispense routine services.

The grand irony of Watergate is the way in which Watergate will prevent future Watergates for a decade, perhaps a generation. Not because it will inspire corrective legislation—though it will—but because politicians rarely make the same mistake twice. (Nixon never repeated the error of waging a fifty-state campaign, as he did in 1960. The meaning of Muskie's 1972 campaign, in which his commitment to enter all state primaries stretched his resources to the diminishing point, is that future candidates will be highly selective, where possible, in choosing their fields of battle. The labor union elements in the Democratic Party, after their defeat by the McGovern forces, will no longer rely on playing a broker's role at future conventions but can be expected to become involved in nomination fights on the precinct level—indeed, it may be that some analysts in 1976 will bemoan the advantages that the party's rules give to the old lib-lab coalition with its shop stewards reaching into every community.) Thus the immediate lesson of Watergate for politicians will be that they must conduct themselves with a cleansing scrupulousness—at least until Watergate sounds as musty as Teapot Dome. While political scientists propose reforms on the basis of yesterday's deficiencies, politicians will be making instant adjustments. Yet there are proposals that professional students of politics should make as their contribution to improving the presidential selection process. The next section of this chapter is one attempt at setting the agenda.

Party Control of the Presidential Selection Process

Watergate provides a sorrowful reminder of how much we miss by not having a strong two-party system with a professional code of ethics for those who participate in the political process. Running presidential campaigns under the centralized control of the parties' national committees will not produce the millennium. American parties practice a type of accommodation politics that is not well suited to injecting creativity into public debate. But it is highly unlikely that the Republican National Committee would seriously consider breaking into the Democratic National Committee, or vice versa, if only for the reason stated by David S. Broder in *The Party's Over:* "Our political parties are old, and they expect to be in business a long time. Neither of them has any great temptation to kick down the walls, or to pursue tactics when temporarily in power that will invite revenge from the opposition when it (inevitably) returns to power."[6]

It is doubtful that the political parties can ever regain the central position in the American system that they held in the nineteenth century. Government has replaced the parties as dispenser of social services, patronage is no longer an attractive enough lure to recruit political workers, other forms of entertainment and voluntary associations now compete with the parties on unequal terms, and television gives the voters increased opportunities to get information and judge candidates outside the party context. But the parties do have it within their power to regain control of presidential campaigns. For they have one lever without which no candidate can expect to become President—a major party line on the voting machines. (Another important lever would be party control over campaign funds.)

The place to begin to assert control is the quadrennial national conventions. Although thought of primarily as the places where presidential candidates are nominated and platforms written, the conventions also are the governing bodies of the political parties. It is at the conventions that the parties' rules are adopted and the national committees' mem-

6. David S. Broder, *The Party's Over* (Harper and Row, 1972), p. 179.

berships are ratified. In theory the national committees are subordinate to the national conventions. The conventions' potential to act as the parties' supreme authority was evident at the 1972 Democratic meeting. Under the McGovern Commission guidelines, the convention excluded Mayor Daley's delegation, a graphic demonstration of its power to discipline even the most mighty local party organization. The same convention also approved increasing the size of the Democratic National Committee in an attempt to come to grips with the question of constituent group representation and voted to convene a 1974 conference, which will consider proposals for restructuring the party apparatus. The Republican Party in recent years has been less willing to seek ways to revitalize its organization, but it cannot allow itself to lag too far behind if the Democratic Party changes win popular acceptance.

Every fourth year the Republican and Democratic national conventions confer upon two individuals the right to seek the presidency. Whether the nominees feel any obligations in return is a question for students of psychology. But there should be obligations. The honor of running for President as a major party choice should be based on past conduct and future expectations. The parties should decree that their nominations will be given to persons who abide by certain rules of conduct while seeking their parties' endorsements and will conduct their election campaigns along prescribed lines. As the keepers of the party seal—with the intrinsic power to refuse it as well as confer it—the national conventions (or their delegated agents) should consider the following types of actions:

Pre-convention conduct. Any person seeking the party's nomination should have to submit financial records to periodic audit and agree to abide by a specific code of conduct; who in the party is authorized to press charges against a candidate for code violations should be spelled out in the party's rules; hearings on code violations should be conducted by a designated body; recommendations for sanctions should be voted upon by the full national committee; various penalties could be imposed, including denial of the party's nomination.

General election conduct. Candidates for the nomination should agree to wage their general election campaign under the aegis of the party's national committee. They also should agree that all monies will be raised and spent by the national committee. The nominee must have the right to choose his own campaign manager, who would be in charge of those aspects of the canvass that directly relate to the candidate— his schedule, the logistics of his travels, personal staff, and that part of the media budget that solely promotes the presidential candidate. All other operations should be controlled by the national chairman. No longer should a presidential candidate be able to make a unilateral decision to overfinance his campaign while the rest of the ticket goes underfinanced. Surplus funds (as in the 1972 Nixon campaign) or other assets (as in the case of McGovern's mailing lists) automatically should be the property of the national parties.

Once the parties asserted control over the presidential selection process, a chain reaction might take place. The national committees, with new and important duties, might begin to attract different sorts of people; instead of being a resting place for ancient political warriors or financial angels, membership might go to those who are willing to fight for the right to participate in making decisions that affect the future of the party. The national chairmanship might be viewed as a legitimate career goal, the top position in the political party profession, rather than a part-time job for a busy public official, or a consolation prize for having been passed over for a vice-presidential nomination, or a symbolic reward for a representative of some constituent group. The national chairman even might begin issuing annual "state of the party" messages, which would report on the progress of platform implementation, fund raising, party programs, and staff activities. Television, commercial or public, could allot time to the parties for this purpose. The national conventions should become ongoing bodies to be reconvened two years after the selection of the presidential nominee to consider the health of the party; delegates should be ex officio members of their states' central committees, with election as a delegate implying a four-year obligation to work on party affairs. Such a scheme would create out of the national conventions and national committees a sort of two-chamber structure for the legislating of party concerns. If Americans are willing to work to rebuild the political parties, there is no shortage of imaginative proposals on ways to accomplish this goal.[7] The wisdom of having political parties long ago ceased to be debatable; they are essential to the governance of free societies.

U.S. Code of Fair Campaign Practices

There is now an inadequately regulated category of campaign activity, which the Watergate hearings taught us to call "dirty tricks." The Fair Campaign Practices Committee, a private organization, exists to measure the morality of candidates, but its sanctions are limited to publicity, and its findings often come too late to be very effective. A U.S. Code should be devised to offer a standard of how we wish our candidates to conduct themselves. As Elliot L. Richardson suggests, the Code also should prohibit certain types of activities, such as:

• Belligerent or obscene phone calls falsely represented to be on behalf of a candidate.

• Disruption of campaign operations or gatherings by paid political operatives.

• Transmission of sensitive political information by paid "political spies."[8]

7. See John S. Saloma III and Frederick H. Sontag, *Parties* (Knopf, 1972).

8. Speech by Elliot L. Richardson at the Appeal of Conscience Foundation Dinner, reported in the *New York Times*, Dec. 12, 1973.

Another approach, suggested by Ralph K. Winter, Jr., would have such a code formulated by the national party chairmen and incorporated into the platforms of each party. Enforcement would be through private mechanisms similar to labor arbitration.[9]

Codes of conduct are modest protectors of the public interest at best. Congress legislated a Code of Ethics for Government Service in 1958, and President Kennedy followed up with an executive order in 1961; both without notably improving the caliber of federal conduct. Nevertheless we must continue to seek ways to remind politicians of our expectations.

Federal Elections Commission

The policing of a U.S. Code of Fair Campaign Practices and the authority to conduct investigations and impose sanctions should be vested in a Federal Elections Commission, an independent body of distinguished citizens, which would inherit the campaign financing regulatory duties now performed by the Comptroller General, the Secretary of the U.S. Senate, and the Clerk of the U.S. House of Representatives. It is hardly sensible public policy to allow employees of the Congress to oversee the campaign spending of their employers as now occurs under the 1971 law. Additionally, the law should be changed to provide the watchdog body with prosecutory powers instead of merely the right to refer suspected violators to the Department of Justice.

Campaign Financing

The most likely legislation to result from the Watergate scandal will be in the area of campaign financing. The recommendation in Chapter 6 covers political activities at all levels,

9. See Ralph K. Winter, Jr., *Watergate and the Law* (American Enterprise Institute for Public Policy Research, 1974), p. 51.

rather than only those of candidates for federal office, and provides sufficient public funds to allow candidates to at least minimally make their positions known to the electorate. Such a system would operate through the political parties with special provisions to cover primary elections. The cost over a four-year election cycle is estimated at $750 million. The federal government's share is 80 percent. States "buying" into this grant-in-aid program would be expected to follow prescribed guidelines, including limitations on private contributions, full disclosure, equitable distribution of funds, and provisions to facilitate registration of voters and the efficient operation of the election machinery. The parties would have the right to raise additional funds through small contributions. The proposal contemplates no limitation on the amounts that could be spent but places strict restrictions on the amounts that could be given.

Widening the Field

The final report of the 44th American Assembly correctly concludes, "The number of people given serious consideration for the Presidency should be larger than at present."[10] Since 1936 only sixty-two Democrats and forty-seven Republicans have received at least 1 percent support for President in the Gallup polls.[11] "Is it conceivable," asks Broder, "that in two generations, this nation of 200 million produced only 109 men and women [nearly all white males] with qualifications to be considered presidential possibilities?"[12]

Americans choose their Presidents from a modest field that consists of the Vice President, governors of large states, members of the U.S. Senate, and an occasional military hero. As

10. American Assembly, *Choosing the President* (1973), p. 4.
11. See Donald R. Matthews, "Presidential Nominations: Process and Outcomes," in James David Barber (ed.), *Choosing the President* (Prentice-Hall, 1974), pp. 39–40.
12. David S. Broder, "A Search for Possible Presidents," *Washington Post*, Dec. 30, 1973.

suggested earlier, it would be preferable to propel more candidates into the presidential on-deck circle through a series of recommending conferences held at the beginning of the election year. Meetings of mayors or of members of the U.S. House of Representatives, for example, would be encouraged by the national committees to propose candidates whose names would be placed in nomination at the national conventions. Candidates also could be nominated by a substantial number of petition signatures. Neither method would confer any convention votes. The aim is simply to endorse additional candidates for convention consideration. Some 90 percent of the persons receiving recognition as "presidential material" in the polls between 1936 and 1972 were holders of public office. The ranks of potential Presidents should not be limited to professional politicians. Educators, labor leaders, business executives, and others should be put forward by associations of their colleagues as people of possible presidential quality. To receive a nomination, however, the non-politician should be tested through an essentially political process as is presently the case.

Model Primary Law

That part of the presidential selection process governed by state primary laws might have been designed by cartoonist Rube Goldberg.[13] For each state conducts its presidential primaries under various, and sometimes contradictory, rules. But though we are amused by the contraptions of a "mad inventor" like Goldberg, we should be less willing to accept the conceptual chaos of a system that produces a major decision in our lives. Our concern need not be esthetics or a longing for order. Rather, as citizens taking seriously our

13. See Robert H. Finch, "Primarily, a Problem," New York Times, April 30, 1972. He writes that "the Presidential primaries have degenerated into a pathetic joke, requiring serious statesmen to act like children playing different games under different rules from state to state."

obligations and trying to make sense of the options we are given, we should be offended that our task is made unnecessarily difficult by the confusions imposed by state laws.

Yet the genius of a Goldberg device is not merely that it makes us laugh but that it works; if all the pulleys and fulcrums performed as pictured, somehow they would produce the desired results. My objection to the national primary, stated earlier, is that it would not work: it would leave the country with weakened parties, a reduced number of serious contenders, and a truncated campaign that would be less likely to test presidential qualities.

What is desperately needed is codification and simplification of the present system. Again, this is an area in which the national parties could be the most effective agents for change. Just as the proliferation of primaries in 1972 was partly a response by the states to comply with new Democratic Party rules, so too could the parties come together to design a model presidential primary law, which the states would be expected to substantially follow if they chose to select national convention delegates by this method.[14]

The basic elements of a model presidential primary law should take the following form:

• A standard definition of who is eligible to vote, preferably prohibiting crossover voting.

• Mandatory ballot listing of all declared or serious candidates, as in the Oregon system. It is rarely the case that voters are choosing convention delegates in the representative sense. Given the media's attention to the presidential contenders, voters should know enough to make a choice between candidates or to choose "none of the above."

• Where the names of candidates for convention delegate

14. A less effective way of seeking codification would be to turn the problem over to the National Conference of Commissioners on Uniform State Laws, a body of lawyers, judges, and law school professors which since 1892 has been drafting model legislation for approval by the states.

appear on the ballot, the ballot should indicate a candidate's presidential preference or state "no preference."

• The winner-take-all outcome of primaries should be replaced with a system of proportional representation. This would encourage contenders to enter primaries and would make the conventions more reflective of the true strengths of the presidential candidates.

• A uniform decision should be reached on whether the primaries are binding and, if so, for how many ballots.

Nominating the Vice-Presidential Candidate

We cannot afford to continue to allow the selection of the vice-presidential candidate to be made as an afterthought, the final act of an exhausted national convention acceding to the recommendation of a tired presidential nominee.

The fact that one in three of our Vice Presidents have been elevated to the presidency attests to the importance of this decision; the experience with recent vice-presidential nominees of both parties attests to how atrociously this decision has been made.

Because of the Eagleton affair in 1972, the Democrats stumbled into a different and superior way of choosing a candidate for Vice President. Having the national convention authorize the national committee to convene two or three weeks after the close of the convention for the purpose of selecting a vice-presidential candidate has a number of advantages. Primarily, it gives the presidential nominee an opportunity to carefully consider his recommendation. It allows time to test the sentiment of party professionals and to sample public opinion through scientific polling; it permits detailed investigations to be made into the backgrounds of potential vice-presidential candidates; it allows potential vice-presidential candidates to wage a sort of mini-campaign by appearing on the leading network TV interview programs and by other means of public exposure; it permits the final session of the national convention to focus solely on the attributes of the presidential nominee; and by giving another responsibility to the national committee, it may have the effect of strengthening the party system.

Such a change, however, must go hand-in-glove with reforms that will assure the representativeness of the national committee. It also should allow the national conventions to have the flexibility to choose the vice-presidential candidate if no purpose is served in a given year for delaying the decision. The underlying premise remains that the presidential nominee should be the key decision-maker in selecting his running-mate. We should be fearful of devising a system that would encourage the nomination of a Vice President who is out of phase with the chief executive. What we must do is find ways that will help the presidential nominee to give the proper time and thought to this crucial choice.[15]

Platforms

The party platform (as David Truman has written) is "generally regarded as a document that says little, binds no one, and is forgotten by politicians as quickly as possible."[16] Why then do delegates to presidential conventions, practical people all, engage in such bloody battles over them? One answer, amply documented by Gerald M. Pomper, is that the record is not nearly so dismal as has been commonly assumed. "Perhaps most comforting to those who believe in

15. Another proposal is to have candidates for President and Vice President seek nominations as a team. See James I. Loeb, "On Nominating a Vice President," *Washington Post*, Jan. 27, 1974. A somewhat different proposal, made by myself, is to expect a presidential contender to announce a list of acceptable running-mates during the preconvention period. See "A Modest Suggestion for Candidate Rockefeller," *Wall Street Journal*, Jan. 18, 1974.

16. David B. Truman, *The Governmental Process* (Knopf, 1951), pp. 282–83.

party integrity," Pomper concludes, "is that only a tenth of the promises are completely ignored."[17] Still another reason why the writing of platforms is not mere finger exercises is that, more than trying to tell the voters what the parties will do for them, the drafters are engaged in a collective bargaining process over the composition of the party. The resultant document allows each group to decide whether it can remain within the coalition.

Defining the perimeters of the parties' composition in terms of issue positions could be more usefully performed at the mid-term party conferences, proposed earlier. If such documents were on hand when the presidential selection process began, the candidates would be expected to indicate areas of agreement and disagreement during their preconvention campaigns. In a sense, the parties, rather than the candidates, would set the agenda for debate. The burden of proof would be on those candidates who argued for different goals and programs. Their selection, of course, would be proof that they had "won" their arguments. The national conventions then would be freed to concentrate on choosing presidential standard-bearers, with perhaps the additional duty of approving short, revised statements of principles.

Communications

A number of thoughtful suggestions have been put forth for improving media coverage of the campaigns:

• Minow, Martin, and Mitchell in *Presidential Television* propose, "The national committee of the opposition party should be given by law an automatic right of response to any presidential radio or television address made during the ten

17. Gerald M. Pomper, *Elections in America* (Dodd, Mead, 1970), p. 159. (Pomper stresses the same point on pp. 186–87.) See also Judith H. Parris, *The Convention Problem* (Brookings Institution, 1972), pp. 109–14.

months preceding a presidential election."[18] The purpose served by this "response time" proposal would be to neutralize the incumbent's usual advantage.

• Section 315 of the Communications Act of 1934—the equal time provision—should be repealed so that radio and television stations will have one less reason for denying free time to major party candidates.

• Fred W. Friendly, the former president of CBS News, has proposed a weekly TV broadcast during campaigns and suggests the title "Whose Ox Is Gored?" He sees this as "a venting mechanism" to "supply a place where all the politicians who feel that their ox has been gored by newspapermen or television and radio men get to meet that person and vice versa . . . [where] pollsters come in and report how they did their work . . . where those thirty-second commercials . . . [are] played and somebody says, 'Now let's . . . examine what that says and doesn't say.' "[19] This suggestion recognizes that there are more players than the candidates in presidential selection politics and that the voters need some method of assessing the products of the others—journalists, pollsters, advertising specialists—who also contribute to the outcomes of elections.

Separate studies of television and newspaper coverage of the 1972 campaign independently conclude that there was a strong bias against dealing with the substance of issues and in favor of treating politics as a horserace. The reporter wants to know who is going to win. Handicappers concentrate on such factors as the state of the track, performance in earlier races, conditioning, and the weight of the jockey. All have parallels in political campaign reporting. Issues primarily are

18. Newton N. Minow, John Bartlow Martin, and Lee M. Mitchell, *Presidential Television* (Basic Books, 1973), p. 161. The authors also propose giving free prime TV time to major presidential candidates during the month before the election.

19. "Government Information: The Media and the Public," transcript of a symposium sponsored by the Woodrow Wilson International Center for Scholars, Washington, D.C., May 20, 1971, pp. 158–60.

considered as they relate to possible outcomes. James Perry, for example, finds that though McGovern announced his "tax reform and redistribution of income" proposal on January 13, 1972, it was not given serious press attention until April 27 (*Wall Street Journal*) and May 7 (*Washington Post*).[20]

The corrective for newspapers in handling campaign stories is to make greater use of reporters with specialized knowledge (economics, foreign policy, and so on), to rotate reporters more often, and to give more attention to cross-candidate coverage, which would focus on how particular issues are being dealt with by all candidates rather than treating the candidates as if each existed in his own space capsule. The problem for television is more systemic. A prime prerequisite for network news is that an event should contain visual conflict. But, to paraphrase a former Vice President, "When you've seen one crowd (or demonstration), you've seen 'em all." The style for visual presentation of campaigns instead of heightening public interest has become a cliché. The definition of conflict should include the conflict of ideas. The complexities of a presidential campaign require longer stories and reportage that relies less heavily on moving pictures. In short, the networks should accept a less patronizing posture toward their viewers: Some pictures are not the equivalent of a thousand words. It is hard to overstate the importance of the news media. They are our greatest leverage for forcing candidates to inject substance into politics.

Separate Federal and State/Local Elections

The U.S. system of government is complicated enough without commingling federal, state, and local elections on one ballot.[21] A variety of campaign spending abuses creep

---

20. James M. Perry, *Us & Them: How the Press Covered the 1972 Election* (Clarkson N. Potter, 1973), pp. 144–45.

21. See Committee for Economic Development, *Modernizing State Government* (New York: CED, 1967), pp. 21–22; CED, *Financing a Better Election System* (1968), p. 30.

into the process because of a failure to separate the various levels of elections. Of greater importance, the lumping together makes it difficult for voters to deal with their concerns in an appropriate and systematic manner. A more constructive way of conducting elections would be to hold contests for federal offices in even-numbered years and for state/local offices in odd-numbered years. This division could lead to a simplified ballot for President, senator, and member of the House of Representatives. The end result might promote party discipline; it certainly would promote a more rational dialogue.

Direct Popular Elections

Whether or not to abolish the Electoral College has been the longest-standing debate in American political science. Excellent books have been written on both sides.[22] Many alternatives have been proposed. Without attempting to review all the arguments, it is only necessary to add in an essay on the presidential selection process that I find no convincing evidence that the direct popular election of President would have any significant impact on the way campaigns are waged. It would not materially change the allocation of a candidate's time, the nature of his appeals, or the type of two-party competition that presently exists.

The Electoral College system almost had a mischievous effect on two recent presidential elections. That it did not is hardly a compelling reason to retain it. Had George Wallace been a mite more popular in 1968 and thus been able to transfer the electoral decision to the House of Representatives, we would have had a President chosen in a highly

22. For a defense of the Electoral College, see Wallace S. Sayre and Judith H. Parris, *Voting for President* (Brookings Institution, 1970). The case for direct elections is presented by Neal R. Peirce, *The People's President* (Simon and Schuster, 1968), and Lawrence D. Longley and Alan G. Braun, *The Politics of Electoral College Reform* (Yale University Press, 1972).

inequitable manner. That people called Electors have been able to cast ballots for President in ways that have nullified the wishes of the voters cannot be defended on any grounds. That different groups gain an advantage through the existence of the Electoral College might be reason for the advantaged to fight to keep what they have, but their arguments must be based on other than equity. That minor parties have less influence under the Electoral College system than if the vote was direct should give reformers pause, if true—but at least one scholar of third-party movements in presidential politics contends that the reverse would be the case.[23]

What the direct election of Presidents would do is replace a complicated, difficult to understand, and potentially divisive system with one that is elegantly simple, provides for a basic equality among voters, and ensures that the winning candidate will be the one who receives the most votes. In a presidential selection process that must be widely believed fair in order to legitimate its outcomes, this would be no small achievement.

Some of these proposals are meant to correct flaws in the system. Others are intended primarily to simplify ways that we now operate. A few are framed in response to the abuses of Watergate, understanding, however, that to the degree Watergate was not caused by mechanistic defects, so too incidents like it cannot be prevented solely by mechanistic improvements, only made less likely.

One effect of Watergate, at least until we can view it with some detachment, is that it tends to overshadow all that came before it. Watergate is our most recent history, and Americans have been accused, quite rightly, of having a short historical memory.

But it is not enough to say that the system has worked because the country has been generally well served by Presi-

23. Daniel A. Mazmanian, *Third Parties in Presidential Elections* (Brookings Institution, 1974), p. 114.

dents in the past, at least in times of crisis. Perhaps we were lucky. Perhaps something has changed or will change. Perhaps there is something about the office that lifts men to greatness, in which case almost any system would produce great Presidents. Still, all our Presidents have not been great. Some of the information the electorate might wish to have to help predict presidential fitness can never be discovered beforehand. There are times when no outstanding candidates are available. No matter how much information is on hand, some Presidents will surprise us, favorably as well as unfavorably. There can be no guarantee that voters will always act wisely, even when the facts are known. Rather we should ask whether the way we go about picking chief executives gives us the knowledge we need to make the best decisions possible.

For this purpose I have attempted here to state the essence of presidential qualities, independent of time and ideology; those qualities—personal, political, and executive—without which a President could not properly function. The executive qualities, the ability to organize and manage large enterprises, are not tested significantly by the system. The political qualities, primarily the ability to gauge public opinion and the skill to win approval for one's programs, are well tested, as we should expect in a system where electoral success depends on the welding of so many diverse groups and interests. It is hard to imagine a President getting elected without having mastered the intricacies of politics. (The problem is that, once elected, he may ignore them.) Observers will differ on whether the system does as well at testing personal qualities—the ability to perform as a public person, honesty and courage, physical stamina, a style that is acceptable to most Americans, the ability to inspire public trust, and a sense of history, meaning "personal loyalty to democratic values." My own view is that, though our method falls short of what we desire, alternative systems would be equally flawed.

Yet my contention is that the process is more than a testing ground. It is equally a training ground. It tells the electorate things they need to know about the candidates, and it teaches the candidates things that will be useful in the White House. In 1960, when campaigning for the Democratic nomination, Kennedy spent a month in West Virginia. This experience, wrote Schlesinger at the time, "gave his social views a new concreteness. He had read a good deal about poverty, but . . . he had never seen fellow countrymen living the way unemployed miners and their families are living today in West Virginia; and the sight struck home with peculiar force."[24] The West Virginia presidential primary, directly and indirectly, produced the Area Redevelopment Act, the Appalachian Regional Commission, and a governmental response to strip mining.

Functioning as a system of personnel selection, the presidential campaign, a long and arduous method of exposing candidates to public scrutiny, has taken on certain aspects of a presidency simulation and—exactly because it is an ordeal —gives the people much necessary data with which to measure politicians, as well as the time to make an assessment.

The system limits our mistakes to four years, allowing us to judge chief executives retrospectively and take corrective action if needed. As a mechanism for policy formulation, the campaign is not creative, precise, or intellectually rigorous; but if it does not bring forth new initiatives, it often grinds fine those that are already in the public arena. The constant repetition of the candidates' basic themes provides information on what they consider important, and through the interaction between candidates and electorate, they get some information on what the voters think is important. The campaign no longer entertains us, as it once did, but it is questionable whether this is any longer a worthwhile function.

The nature of the campaign has changed remarkably little in the twentieth century. It still produces the same types of

24. Arthur M. Schlesinger, Jr., *Kennedy or Nixon: Does It Make Any Difference?* (Macmillan, 1960), p. 27.

candidates; basically it is a screening process for professional politicians. Other professions may produce persons of greater intelligence, integrity, or executive ability, and they should be tested, too. But it is doubtful that they would as closely fit the unique—if unattractive—set of personal and political qualities that are the presidential "constants." Television— the most notable addition to the tools of communications— must have long-term consequences on the viewers' expectations, acceptance of public officials, and menu of issues, but it has had surprisingly little impact in the short run on who gets nominated or elected. After two decades of experience, we are no more "manipulated" than we were before TV campaigning. Television and other factors add to the cost of running for the presidency. This has not deterred any otherwise viable candidates from seeking the office; nor, on the other hand, has any candidate been able to "buy" a nomination or election. Campaign financing raises troubling and serious problems; fortunately, however, they are susceptible to corrective legislation.

Besides the need to create a rational system of campaign financing, the most pressing need at this time is for a more disciplined party structure to contain the selection process. This does not mean that many of the other persistent criticisms of the system are necessarily wrong so much as that they are often esthetic rather than political judgments. The remedy, as Justice Holmes said about evils in general, may be "to grow more civilized." Yet this is not a matter that can be imposed by statute. Moreover, some of the proposals for change might be good esthetics and bad democratic procedure. Efforts to shorten the campaign, for example, would reduce the boredom while further handicapping the underdog candidate (usually the challenger) and those voters who need the most time to reach a decision (usually the underclass). More serious is the concern over the platitudinous nature of political discourse. Herbert Stein, an adviser to President Nixon, once said that during election campaigns "there is a certain depreciation of the verbal currency which goes on, which everyone seems to understand and discount and which apparently does no harm."[25] He is mistaken in saying that it does no harm. Voting must depend on "the verbal currency," and candidates constantly must be reminded that we hold them accountable. Here, as I have indicated, the press deserves some of the blame: fascinated by the political maneuverings of the candidates, newspaper and television reporters have been distracted from adequately analyzing the candidates' stands on issues.

It is therefore possible to agree with many of the criticisms of the way Presidents are chosen—it is vulgar, it does debase the language, it is costly and wasteful and chaotic, it is a bore—and still conclude that the system provides a remarkably thorough way to learn those things that are learnable about the people who seek the presidency. It may be that campaigns show candidates at their worst. We would also like to know their best. But if we cannot know both, it is more useful to know the worst. At a time when national disillusion is becoming a minor art form, it is instructive to remind ourselves that this is considerably more than cold comfort.

25. James L. Rowe, Jr., "Stein Sees Need for Big Economic Planning Agency," *Washington Post*, Dec. 30, 1973.

Bibliography

THIS BIBLIOGRAPHY is meant to be highly selective. It is primarily designed for the reader who may be delving into the topic of presidential selection for the first time and has become engaged enough to wish to pursue that new interest. For more specialized citations, see the footnotes that accompany this essay.

The Presidency

Bailey, Thomas A. *Presidential Greatness*. New York: Appleton-Century, 1966.

Barber, James David. *The Presidential Character*. Englewood Cliffs, N.J.: Prentice-Hall, 1972.

Binkley, Wilfred E. *The Man in the White House*. Baltimore: Johns Hopkins Press, 1958.

Brownlow, Louis. *The President and the Presidency*. Chicago: Public Administration Service, 1949.

Corwin, Edward S. *The President: Office and Powers, 1787–1957*. New York: New York University Press, 1957.

Finer, Herman. *The Presidency: Crisis and Regeneration*. Chicago: University of Chicago Press, 1960.

Hargrove, Erwin C. *Presidential Leadership*. New York: Macmillan, 1966.

Herring, Pendleton. *Presidential Leadership*. New York: Farrar and Rinehart, 1940.

Hughes, Emmet John. *The Living Presidency*. New York: Coward, McCann and Geoghegan, 1973.

Hyman, Sidney. *The American President*. New York: Harper, 1954.

Kallenbach, Joseph E. *The American Chief Executive*. New York: Harper and Row, 1966.

Koenig, Louis W. *The Chief Executive*. Rev. ed. New York: Harcourt, Brace and World, 1968.

Laski, Harold J. *The American Presidency*. New York: Harper, 1940.

Neustadt, Richard E. *Presidential Power*. New York: Wiley, 1960.

Reedy, George. *The Twilight of the Presidency*. New York: World, 1970.

Roseboom, Eugene H. *A History of Presidential Elections*. New York: Macmillan, 1957.

Rossiter, Clinton. *The American Presidency*. New York: Harcourt, Brace and World, 1960.

Schlesinger, Arthur M., Jr. *The Imperial Presidency*. Boston: Houghton Mifflin, 1973.

Sorensen, Theodore E. *Decision-Making in the White House*. New York: Columbia University Press, 1963.

Wildavsky, Aaron (ed.). *The Presidency*. Boston: Little, Brown, 1969.

Franklin D. Roosevelt

Burns, James MacGregor. *Roosevelt: The Lion and the Fox*. New York: Harcourt, Brace and World, 1956.

————. *Roosevelt: The Soldier of Freedom*. New York: Harcourt Brace Jovanovich, 1970.

Rosenman, Samuel I. *Working with Roosevelt*. New York: Harper, 1952.

Schlesinger, Arthur M., Jr. *The Age of Roosevelt*. Vol. 1: *The Crisis of the Old Order*. Vol. 2: *The Coming of the New Deal*. Vol. 3: *The Politics of Upheaval*. Boston: Houghton Mifflin, 1957, 1958, 1960.

Sherwood, Robert E. *Roosevelt and Hopkins*. New York: Harper, 1948.

Tugwell, Rexford G. *The Democratic Roosevelt*. Garden City, N.Y.: Doubleday, 1957.

Harry S. Truman

Miller, Merle. *Plain Speaking: An Oral Biography of Harry S. Truman*. New York: Berkley, 1974.

Phillips, Cabell. *The Truman Presidency*. New York: Macmillan, 1966.

Truman, Margaret. *Harry S. Truman*. New York: Morrow, 1972.

Truman, Harry S. *Memoirs*. Vol. 1: *Year of Decisions*. Vol. 2: *Years of Trial and Hope*. Garden City, N.Y.: Doubleday, 1955, 1956.

Dwight D. Eisenhower

Adams, Sherman. *Firsthand Report*. New York: Harper, 1961.
Eisenhower, Dwight D. *The White House Years*. Vol. 1: *Mandate for Change, 1953–1956*. Vol. 2: *Waging Peace, 1956–1961*. Garden City, N.Y.: Doubleday, 1963, 1965.
Hughes, Emmet John. *The Ordeal of Power*. New York: Atheneum, 1963.
Larson, Arthur. *Eisenhower: The President Nobody Knew*. New York: Scribner's, 1968.
Parmet, Herbert S. *Eisenhower and the American Crusades*. New York: Macmillan, 1972.

John F. Kennedy

Burns, James MacGregor. *John Kennedy: A Political Profile*. New York: Harcourt, Brace, 1959.
Fairlie, Henry. *The Kennedy Promise*. Garden City, N.Y.: Doubleday, 1973.
Salinger, Pierre. *With Kennedy*. Garden City, N.Y.: Doubleday, 1966.
Schlesinger, Arthur M., Jr. *A Thousand Days*. Boston: Houghton Mifflin, 1965.
Sorensen, Theodore C. *Kennedy*. New York: Harper and Row, 1965.

Lyndon B. Johnson

Evans, Rowland, and Robert Novak. *Lyndon B. Johnson: The Exercise of Power*. New York: New American Library, 1966.
Goldman, Eric F. *The Tragedy of Lyndon Johnson*. New York: Knopf, 1969.
Johnson, Lyndon B. *The Vantage Point*. New York: Holt, Rinehart and Winston, 1971.
McPherson, Harry C. *A Political Education*. Boston: Atlantic–Little, Brown, 1972.

Richard M. Nixon

Evans, Rowland, and Robert Novak. *Nixon in the White House.* New York: Random House, 1971.

Mazlish, Bruce. *In Search of Nixon.* New York: Basic Books, 1972.

Mazo, Earl, and Stephen Hess. *Nixon: A Political Portrait.* Rev. ed. New York: Harper and Row, 1969.

Nixon, Richard M. *Six Crises.* Garden City, N.Y.: Doubleday, 1962.

Wills, Garry. *Nixon Agonistes.* New York: New American Library, 1970.

Witcover, Jules. *The Resurrection of Richard Nixon.* New York: Putnam, 1970.

The Presidential Campaign of 1956

Stevenson, Adlai E. *The New America.* New York: Harper, 1957.

Thomson, Charles A. H., and Frances M. Shattuck. *The 1956 Presidential Campaign.* Washington: Brookings Institution, 1960.

The Presidential Campaign of 1960

David, Paul T. (ed.). *The Presidential Election and Transition, 1960–1961.* Washington: Brookings Institution, 1961.

Kraus, Sidney (ed.). *The Great Debates.* Gloucester, Mass.: Peter Smith, 1968.

Schlesinger, Arthur M., Jr. *Kennedy or Nixon: Does It Make Any Difference?* New York: Macmillan, 1960.

White, Theodore H. *The Making of the President 1960.* New York, Atheneum, 1961.

The Presidential Campaign of 1964

Cummings, Milton C., Jr. (ed.). *The National Election of 1964.* Washington: Brookings Institution, 1966.

Gilder, George F., and Bruce K. Chapman. *The Party That Lost Its Head.* New York: Knopf, 1966.

Hess, Karl. *In a Cause That Will Triumph: The Goldwater Campaign and the Future of Conservatism.* Garden City, N.Y.: Doubleday, 1969.

Kessel, John H. *The Goldwater Coalition.* Indianapolis: Bobbs-Merrill, 1968.

Shadegg, Stephen. *What Happened to Goldwater?* New York: Holt, Rinehart and Winston, 1965.

White, Theodore H. *The Making of the President 1964.* New York: Atheneum, 1965.

The Presidential Campaign of 1968

Chester, Lewis, Godfrey Hodgson, and Bruce Page. *An American Melodrama.* New York: Viking, 1969.

McCarthy, Eugene J. *The Year of the People.* Garden City, N.Y.: Doubleday, 1969.

McGinniss, Joe. *The Selling of the President 1968.* New York: Trident, 1969.

Polsby, Nelson W. *The Citizen's Choice, Humphrey or Nixon.* Washington: Public Affairs Press, 1968.

White, Theodore H. *The Making of the President 1968.* New York: Atheneum, 1969.

The Presidential Campaign of 1972

Cannon, Lou. *The McCloskey Challenge.* New York: Dutton, 1972.

Crouse, Timothy. *The Boys on the Bus.* New York: Random House, 1973.

Dougherty, Richard. *Goodbye, Mr. Christian: A Personal Account of McGovern's Rise and Fall.* Garden City, N.Y.: Doubleday, 1973.

Ferguson, James R., and Marc F. Plattner. *Report on Network News' Treatment of the 1972 Democratic Presidential Candidates.* Bloomington, Ind.: Alternative Educational Foundation, 1972.

Mailer, Norman. *St. George and the Godfather.* New York: New American Library, 1972.

May, Ernest R., and Janet Fraser (eds.). *Campaign '72.* Cambridge, Mass.: Harvard University Press, 1973.

Perry, James M. *Us & Them: How the Press Covered the 1972 Election.* New York: Clarkson N. Potter, 1973.

Thompson, Hunter S. *Fear and Loathing: On the Campaign Trail '72.* New York: Popular Library, 1973.

White, Theodore H. *The Making of the President 1972.* New York: Atheneum, 1973.